My Father's Guiding Hand

A True Story of God's Grace and Faithfulness

My Father's Guiding Hand

A True Story of God's Grace and Faithfulness

M. Gloria Meiusi

REDEMPTION
PRESS

Published by Redemption Press, PO Box 427, Enumclaw, WA 98022, Toll Free (844) 2REDEEM (273-3336)

Redemption Press is honored to present this title in partnership with the author. The views expressed or implied in this work are those of the author. Redemption Press provides our imprint seal representing design excellence, creative content and high quality production.

ISBN 13: 978-1-63232-803-8 (Print)
        978-1-63232-804-5 (ePub)
        978-1-63232-809-0 (Mobi)

Library of Congress Catalog Card Number: 2015959968

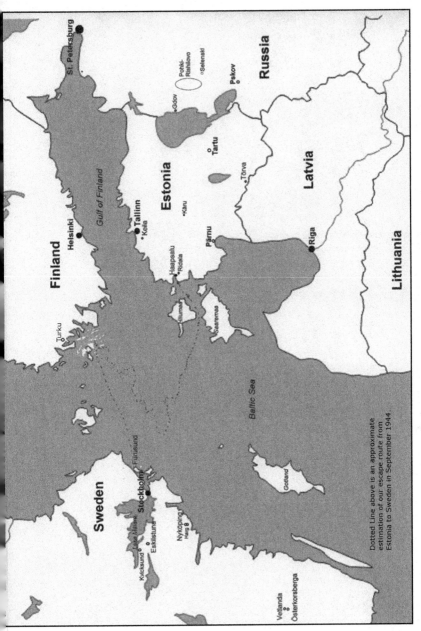

Map courtesy of http://d-maps.com/pays.php?num_pay=182&lang=en,
accessed on January 21, 2016.

Dedication

I dedicate this book with a grateful and humble heart in memory of my parents, but especially to my father, Victor Konsa. While writing this, I came to a new realization of how my father's guiding hand has had such a loving and positive impact on my life in showing me the clear way to my heavenly Father.

I also dedicate this to our grandchildren: (in the order of their ages) Elizabeth Mairi, Peter Jacob, Katrin Ruth, Jonathan Abel, Anna Grace, Molly Adele, Abigail Joanna, Monica Kirsten, and Caroline Joy.

It was when I used to speak and give my testimony in many Christian Women's Clubs and to different organizations and churches that people asked me over and over, "Have you written a book about your life?"

I would reply, "Maybe someday when I'm a grandmother I'll have more time to do that . . ."

As our grandchildren were growing, they begged me to tell them bedtime stories, and I told them stories of "when I was a little girl." Later they started saying, "Mamma, you need to write these stories down!"

Years passed and, finally, here is the first part of my life story written so that children could read some of the personal experiences that God allowed me to go through—some happy and funny—others rather hard and painful. It covers my life up to the time I met and married by dear husband, Endel Meiusi. I am now in the process of writing a follow-up to this book about our life together.

I thank my sisters, Hulda Eistrat and Esther Kaups, for helping me recall some of the events from our childhood and Esther's husband, Taavi Kaups, for some of the political facts and other information. Many thanks also to our daughter, Lillian Tamm, for doing some of the editing and helping to choose the pictures. She gave the final push through her college friend, Valerie Jones-McKay of Redemption Press, Inc. to actually get this into print.

My prayer is that my story will bring glory to God and will impress on your heart the value of both physical and spiritual freedom. I hope it will be a blessing to each one who reads it.

Contents

Preface

To help readers understand the names of my brother, sister, and myself used in the book, I'd like to explain that in America my brother and sister are known as Dave and Esther, and I by my given middle name, Gloria. But before we came to America and even today when we are with Estonians and at home, we use our given first names: Kaljo, Ester, and Mairy.

Chapter 1

Looking Back ᴄ∕ᴖ

The sun is shining brightly on this clear Friday afternoon. It is the sixth of June, 1986. Standing on the deck of the ferry *Georg Ots* on the Baltic Sea with the wind blowing through my hair, I can barely see the coastline of Estonia way out in the distance. Estonia. The land of my birth that I had to leave as a child so many years ago. Tears well up in my eyes; I have thought I would never return and even now I have such mixed emotions since the Russians are still occupying my little nation. My thoughts cannot help but drift back to my childhood . . .

I was born at home in Ridala, Estonia, nine kilometers from the town of Haapsalu on a cold snowy winter Wednesday, the twenty-fourth of January, 1934. Since both of my older siblings, Hulda Marie and Ester Elisabeth, were girls, my mother had longed for a boy. "Papa," as we always called my father, who along with a mid-wife assisted with my birth, later told me that as he held me up and announced the birth of another girl, Mamma turned her head in disappointment.

Later when the rush of my birth was over and everything had settled down, Papa had opened the Bible on the nightstand and the verse popped open where God says He is not a respecter of persons but loves us all (paraphrased from Romans 2:11). Mamma had turned her head back to Papa with a big smile and they both thanked the Creator of all life, especially for this new little girl whom they named Mairy Marta Gloria Konsa (Konsa was our family name).

Ours was a happy home, filled with love, joy, and peace. We lived in the parsonage of the Ridala Baptist Church, which was housed at the back of the church building. There were two rooms on the main floor, a kitchen, hallway, pantry, and a dry-closet ("bathroom," which was occasionally cleaned out from the outside cellar). Across the hall one could step right into the big sanctuary which, including the balcony in the back, could hold many hundreds of people.

The large front room of our home was partitioned off by a tall closet on one side and Papa's desk with a bookcase that reached almost to the ceiling on the other side with a curtain between that "closed" this area as a "doorway." The bookcase was filled with all kinds of theological, religious and medical books, encyclopedias, dictionaries, etc. This front part of the room formed Papa's office but was actually called the "*vendade tuba*" or brethren's room.

Every Sunday morning the elders and pastor (our Papa) met in this room for prayer and used it at other times for board meetings or discussions, interviews with new members-to-be, counseling, and so on. Papa's medicine cabinet was also in this room. People would come to seek medical help instead of going to a doctor in Haapsalu since Papa had studied medicine in Germany before studying at seminary and going into the ministry. With his medical background and compassionate heart, coming to him for medical care often seemed natural for the people.

Behind the tall closet in the other part of this front room was a double bed that we called "*kuld voodi*" or the "golden bed," made of shiny gold-colored brass where my sisters slept. There was also enough room here for a wardrobe.

In the second room slept Papa, Mamma, and I, and this is where I was born! Besides the beds, dresser, table, chairs, and nightstand, on the other side of this room stood a huge oven heated by wood. Even now I can almost smell the fresh loaves of bread as Mamma would take them out of the oven on baking days! Since during cold weather and winter months the huge oven had to be heated anyway, besides baking bread, Mamma roasted potatoes, meats, and many different dishes, some in clay pots, like barley or bread puddings. The food preparation, however, was done right next door in the kitchen.

The kitchen consisted of a wood-heated stove for cooking and heating water, a table, chairs, some cupboards, and a side table with a dishpan for doing the dishes that was replaced with a washbowl where we could wash ourselves. During the winter, this is where we also took our baths when a tub was brought in on the floor, or sometimes we went to a neighbor's sauna. In warmer weather, we washed outside in a private area near the well. Water for the house had to be hand pumped from the outside well before being carried several meters to the building, up the eight stone steps, and down the hall by the kitchen door where it was kept for use in buckets on a covered shelf (and all wastewater was carried out the same way). Of course, this was no luxury living, but we never heard our parents complain about all the disadvantages of living in a "fishbowl." People from our church could walk in at any time and feel that they were always welcome. Strangers could find rest and encouragement here, and Mamma always had some hot tea or coffee to offer to anyone who came by.

Backside of the Ridala Baptist Church where we lived 1933-1944

Front side of the Ridala Baptist
Church and main entrance

Our family 1935: Ester, Papa,
Mamma, Mairy, Hulda

On Sunday mornings, especially during the winter
months, the ladies gathered in the warm kitchen by

the stove to dry out their long skirts, coats, and boots after walking through the snow on their way to church. So we all had to be dressed, finished with breakfast, and ready for the day before the whole place was "invaded." This was just part of the routine. We had lots of "routines."

Each morning we would sing our "morning song:" "*Kui unest üles ärkan ja silmad lahti teen, Siis laulan sulle Looja ja kiidan Isa Sind. Et oled öösel hoidnud, mind kõige kahju eest, Sa ise oled valvan'd, kui mina magasin.*" (Loose translation: When I awake in the morning and open wide my eyes, I'll sing to you, Creator, and praise You, God Most High; that through the night You've held me and kept me from all harm. So lovingly You watched me, when I was sleeping still.)

At mealtimes we had several songs and prayers, such as, "*Oh, Issand Jeesus tule, Meil ise võõraks ole, Sa meile lauda kata, Kõik õnnistada võta, Amen.*" Oh, come Lord Jesus, and be our guest, supply our table and make it blessed!" We also said a similar prayer in German, "*Komm Herr Jesus, sei unser Gast und segne was Du uns gegeben hast, Amen.*" In fact, quite often we had a "rule" that we could only speak German during mealtime, so to this day I would never go hungry in Germany for lack of knowing how to ask, "*Bitte gib mir Brot, Bitte gib mir Kartoffeln, Bitte gib mir Butter, etc.*" (Please give me bread, potatoes, butter), but for each thing, we always said "please" and of course "dankeshön" (thank you).

Discipline was very consistently and lovingly practiced in our home. Papa had lived in Germany for ten years and studied at a Christian medical school, where each part of the day and each chore was done properly and distinctly. More later about Papa, whose name was Victor Konsa and Mamma, named Adele Sünd.

Most evenings when Papa was home we would gather around the harmonium as he played and led in singing. Papa taught all of us girls how to play chords on the harmonium, a little organ pumped with your feet. As we grew older, Mamma taught us to play chords on the zither, so we would often play along with instruments as we sang. After our singing time, we read the Bible and then we always knelt, each of us praying out loud. This was followed by the final evening prayer-song (which we've passed down to our children and grandchildren), "*Mind tiiva alla võta, Oh Jeesus hästi kata, Su kanapojukest. Kui kuri tahab neelda, siis lase inglid keelda. See laps peab jääma rahule, Amen.*" ("Take me under your wing, and cover me, oh Jesus, Your little baby-chick. Lest harm would me now swallow, bid angels to protect me. This child shall go to sleep in peace.") There were many other evening songs as well. One favorite, especially during summer evenings as we watched the sun go down, was "*Õhtupäike veereb metsa taha*" ("The evening sun is sinking down behind the forest"), or when there was lighting and thunder, we would sing "How Great Thou Art" ("*Suur oled Sa*"), since one verse speaks of the greatness of God in thunder and lightning. ("*Kui kõue mürin minu kõrvu kostub ja pikse nooled õhus lendavad . . .*")

My earliest childhood memories are of how I would wake up and start singing in my bed. Mamma told me many times that I brought her so much joy, as I was always happy, laughing, and singing.

I really looked up to Hulda and Ester—they were my big sisters, and especially if Hulda said anything, it *had* to be right.

The whole family had great times singing together, and if I didn't know a certain song well enough, I would "direct" our family "choir," making them sing it over and over while waving my hands rhythmically until I, too, had the song memorized. God had given each of us a natural ability to harmonize. Ester sang the alto part, Hulda and Mamma sang the melody, I usually sang an octave higher or sang the descant (or tenor two octaves higher), and Papa sang bass.

While the church choir was practicing either in the sanctuary or during colder weather upstairs, since during the week the sanctuary was usually not heated, we heard all the different parts being taught separately as well as together. We sang the men's parts an octave or two higher, making it easy for us to just follow along. To this day, whenever we three girls are together, we spontaneously break into some great choir anthem and sing in different parts. Most of the time while Mamma was doing her daily chores she also hummed a tune or joyfully sang out loud, so how else could we even live a day except with a song in our hearts?

If the sun was shining in the morning, Papa would open the drapes and say, "We're not the children of darkness, but children of Light! – so let the sun shine in!" Right away, one of us would strike up a song either about letting our light shine, being sunbeams for Jesus, having sunlight in our souls today, or some other happy song, and so the day began with praises to our heavenly Father! The abundance of praise for every little thing was taught and practiced in our home. What a heritage!

Chapter 2

My Heritage

On my father's side, my great-grandfather, Peter Konsa, was born in 1825 on Õssu Farm near Tartu, Estonia. He and his wife, Amalia, had four sons and one daughter. My grandfather Hendrik (1849-1898), who was born at Tähtvere (also near Tartu), was their second son. Hendrik married Maria (Mari) Maaser, the youngest of nine children (1852-1919) from a devout Lutheran family that lived outside of Tartu at Kambja on a farm. My grandmother Maria's father's name was Hans. Maria was confirmed as a teenager. To my grandparents, Hendrik and Maria, ten children were born, with my father, Peter Victor Konsa, being their last child (April 29, 1892 - May 27, 1974).

At that time, Estonia was under the rule of the Czarist Russian Empire and was a Russian province until 1917, so migrating from one area to the other required no border formalities or clearances. Tartu, located on the Estonian side of Lake Peipsi in eastern Estonia, was not that far from Russia. As the czar was offering good fertile land to Estonian landowners, three of the Konsa brothers, Hendrik (my grandfather) with his family, and his brothers Jaan and Mihkel, made the decision to move east and settle in a place called Pohki, Oudova District in 1869-70.

Pohki became a thriving Estonian village. Each of the brothers bought a farm and Hendrik bought a large estate from the widow of an Orthodox priest who no longer could manage it alone. The Konsa family farmed there for several years, but since Hendrik had had a flour mill near Emajõgi by Tartu before, he longed to live on a river and run a flour mill.

When a suitable piece of land became available in a settlement called Rishilovo, the family bought it and moved to this beautiful location where the river curves and winds through rolling hills and meadows. Here Hendrik and his family built a flour mill on the Lütta River and all the buildings necessary for a farm. The house and other buildings were placed along the riverfront.

The mill proved to be very profitable. Rishilovo was an Estonian settlement of about 300 Estonian families, but Russians from miles around also came to the flour mill. An Estonian Lutheran church with a primary school had been built, and the children attended there. Russian was also taught so everyone learned the local language fluently, but Estonian, the mother tongue, was always spoken in all Estonian homes.

My grandmother Maria was very religious and before my father was born, she had dedicated him to the Lord with a prayer that this child would one day become a servant of God. Even at an early age, my father loved to sing songs about Jesus with his mother and before the age of six was reading fluently from the big family Bible written in Gothic letters. Papa related to me how his mother had told him about how most of their family had become believers: The Konsa family had heard that some Estonian preachers and brethren in St. Petersburg and Selenski were holding meetings and also visiting other Estonian communities. Even though these cities were some distance away, by word of mouth they had heard that many people had become born-again Christians and were completely changed. Most of these Estonians were Lutherans in name only, frequently drinking, carousing, and stealing, but they had become honest and respectable people.

So my grandparents, Hendrik and Maria, were very curious about what these men were preaching and how these changes had happened. They sent two of their older children, Aleksander and Roosi, to go investigate and ask if perhaps these Christian men could also come and preach in Rishilovo. The two returned home with the news that these were truly men of God and they would try to come as soon as time permitted.

Some time went by, and one day as my grandmother Maria was cooking dinner for her big family, she happened to look out the window and saw two strangers walking towards their house. She went out to welcome these guests and sure enough, they were the Christian brethren who had received the invitation to come for a visit. She happily invited them in and showed them to the front room to relax until dinner was ready. As she went about preparing, from the next room she heard these two men start praying out loud and after that start singing a beautiful song:

"*Me reisime ülesse õndsate maale,*
Kus lõpmata armastus ühendab meid . . ."

and the chorus kept repeating:

"*Tahte ka reisida, Tahte ka reisida?*
Kas tahate Taevasse reisida ka?"

(translation): "We're traveling upward to the heavenly country, Where endless love binds us together . . ." (chorus), "Do you also want to travel? Do you want to travel? Do you want to travel to heaven with us?" This touched the heart of my grandmother so deeply that with tears streaming down her cheeks, she fell to her knees and started singing softly with the guests in the next room: "Yes, yes, I also want to travel to heaven with you."

Within the next few days, both of my grandparents, five of their nine living children, and several of their neighbors became born again believers. My father was three years old at the time and was down on his knees with the rest of them, but he did not actually receive the Lord until later.

When Papa was six years old, his father became very ill with pneumonia. At the end, he gathered all his children to his bedside, laid hands on them, and blessed each one before he peacefully went to be with his Maker.

Papa has told us that his mother had very vividly related the events of her husband's illness to him. She told of how one night in a dream when Hendrik was on his sickbed, he had seen a cross with Jesus hanging on it. He had watched different men pounding nails into the body of Jesus, and then he too had picked up a hammer and started pounding nails just like the others, into Jesus! With this vivid dream he had awakened, crying out to Jesus, "No, no, never will I pound nails into your body! Please forgive me for any sin that I have ever committed, forgive me, forgive me!" After this dream, as he still lay in his bed with pneumonia, the Holy Spirit filled him to overflowing, and he started praising God, giving all glory to Him. He was like a different man with great joy on his countenance.

Soon after that night, after he had blessed all his children, my grandmother had been sitting close to his bed when he looked up to heaven and said, "Do you see the two men who are coming for me?"

When she said, "No, I don't see anyone," he responded, "Of course you cannot see them! They are coming to take me to heaven!" Then he had squeezed her hand and with a peaceful, yet joyful face, closed his eyes and, at the age of forty-nine, was gone. He had had a very loving relationship with his wife and there was much caring and love in the family. Wonderful and blessed memories of their godly father lingered on.

Some years after their father's death, most of the family moved back to Estonia where my father received his high school education in Tallinn, at the Westholm Gümnaasium. There among other subjects, he learned German. While living in Tallinn, he committed his life fully to God, was baptized, and in 1912 traveled to Germany for further study at the Mennonite-supported Christian Evangelistic Bible and Missionary School at Bahnau, a small town a couple of miles from the town of Heilingenbeil.[1]

Papa received a good education in Bible subjects and practical Christian living there. The students earned their keep by doing maintenance and gardening so Papa also gained much knowledge about growing vegetables and flowers that was useful even later in life.

Not long after World War I broke out in the summer of 1914, Papa and the other students at the school were sent to work in hospitals. At the time, Estonia was still part of Czarist Russia. In the late winter of 1917, a parliamentary revolution in Russia ended the Czarist government.

My Heritage

The following autumn the communist revolution in Russia overthrew Russia's fledgling democratic government. Russian participation in World War I ended with the Brest - Litovsk Treaty[2] between communist Russia and Germany in March 1918. Estonia declared its independence on February 24, 1918, but that February, Germany had occupied Estonia. World War I ended in the West in November 1918, but Estonia's war of independence from Russia began in earnest as the Germans retreated from the country. Peace did not come until the Tartu Peace Treaty was signed between Estonia and Soviet Russia on February 2, 1920.

Papa continued his studies in Germany, including studying medicine while working in a hospital in Posen for several years. While Papa was in Germany, his beloved, praying mother, who was living in Tallinn, died on January 2, 1919, at age sixty-seven and she is buried in Rahumäe Cemetery in Tallinn.

During the ten years he lived in Germany, Papa felt the call of God to return to his homeland to further his education for pastoral ministry. In 1921, he enrolled in the Estonian Baptist Seminary in Keila where he was a good student, played the trumpet, violin, and the harmonium, sang in the choir, and was active in many school activities. Papa was a slender, fine-boned, handsome man, nearly 5'11" tall with dark brown hair, blue eyes, a high forehead, and a gentle and friendly countenance. As a young man, he wore a small moustache.

Maria Konsa, Papa's
Mother 1907

Peter Victor Konsa
(Papa) 1924, age 32

Marie & Rein Sünd's family 1907 (Marie holding Minda,
Adele, Rein, Robert with Leo in the back)

My Heritage

Adele Marie Sünd (Mamma) 1924, age 23

On my mother's side, my grandfather's name was Rein Sünd (February 23, 1866 – February 1948). He was born into a family of six daughters and he was the only son. His father, my great-grandfather, was named Hans (1840-1903). When my grandfather was three years old, my great-grandmother, Madle (Tomsen) Sünd (1839-1868) at age twenty-eight, along with my grandfather Rein's two sisters Liso and Liisu, were murdered by robbers who broke into the house while father (my great-grandfather Hans) was away. Little Rein crawled into the oven and was undetected and spared. Hans married again, and his second wife's name was Eedu (Poots) Sünd (1843). They had more daughters.

They lived in Asuküla, Läänemaa, in the southwest part of Estonia. Rein gave his heart to the Lord during a revival in Ridala when he was fourteen years old. Later he was one of the founding members of the new Ridala Church. He married Maria Sharbrook and they had one son named Leobolt (1887), or Leo for short. As he grew, he was very artistic; he drew house plans and studied to become an architect. He had light brown wavy hair and a great sense of humor. He was adventuresome and wanted to see the world.

My grandfather Rein's first wife died after only a few years of marriage and since he was left with little Leo, he soon married Marie Remmelman who was exactly ten years younger than he was, having been also born on February 23, but in 1876 (she lived until January 17, 1949). Marie had three sisters and two brothers. They lived in Sutlepa, Läänemaa. Her father's name was Aadu and her mother, who had also been born on February 23 but in 1834, was named Ann or Anna (maiden name Grenzmann). These are my great-grandparents on my mother's side. An interesting side note: My great-grandmother Ann was born exactly 100 years (minus one month and one day) before I was.

Three children were born to my maternal grandparents, Rein and Marie Sünd: Adele Marie, Robert, and Minda Salome. Adele, the eldest (July 22, 1901 - June 27, 1995) was my mother. Robert, three years younger than my mother, was killed at age thirteen when he and a friend climbed on an open freight train and he fell under it. That was quite a tragedy for their family. Robert is buried at the old Ridala cemetery in the same cemetery plot where his parents (my grandparents) were buried many years later, and at the foot of his grave stands a little stone bench that he used to sit on. My aunt Minda was three years younger than Robert. When Adele and the rest of the younger children were born, the family lived in Käru, in Juuru County of Estonia where my grandfather Rein managed a large manor house.

From Käru they moved to Tallinn and lived on Püssirohu Street. Mamma told us that since Estonia was still under the Russian Czarist rule, all of the children were forced to speak Russian in school and a red ribbon was hung around the neck of any child who was caught speaking Estonian. As punishment, the wearer of the red ribbon had to learn extra Russian poetry. The children all spied on each other so they could pass the red ribbon on to someone else, since no one wanted to learn more Russian poetry.

When Adele was about twelve, they moved back to Läänemaa where their roots were, specifically to Parila Manor. Since her father was a very trustworthy man, he was again put in charge of managing the manor house. In about 1922 they bought a farm at Vätsa, about sixteen kilometers south of Haapsalu.

Earlier, a mighty revival had taken place around Ridala, (my birthplace) and in the whole region, which is known to this day among Estonian believers as the "Läänemaa Ärkamine" (Läänemaa Revival, around 1879). My grandmother had come to Christ during the revival years and my grandparents were both members of the Ridala Baptist Church.

As Adele grew and continued going to school, she was a very bright student with a sharp mind. She had an outgoing personality, was involved in the drama club since she had stage presence and great talent in acting and singing, and was a leader and an articulate speaker. She had light brown slightly wavy hair, gray-green eyes, and beautiful skin. Adele was also quick with her fingers and at one point won a potato-peeling contest. As a teenager, she gave her heart to the Lord, was baptized, and became active in the church. The church elders saw that Adele had great potential if she had further education, and she was awarded a scholarship to the Baptist Seminary in Keila.

It was 1921 and the seminary had just opened its doors for the first class of students for studies in theology and related subjects. Besides all the classes and activities at school, Mamma led girls' Bible studies, was involved in mission outreaches and music through the choir, and played guitar in the string orchestra. She also learned to speak English and continued studying German in seminary.

This is where my father and mother met! There was no dating as such allowed while at seminary, but after four years, when graduation drew near, Mamma received two proposals. The first was from one of the students who told her that God told him to ask for her hand in marriage. Well, Mamma had had no such "message" from God, so she said no. The second came from another student who had the same story, but since this time Mamma felt the same way, she accepted Papa's proposal.

Originally, Mamma had not been all that enamored with Papa. He always seemed to be coming to meals late, still buttoning his shirt or fixing something, and Mamma found that frustrating. She felt, however, that as he was a Christian brother, she should pray that she could be more loving and patient towards him. Seems that the Lord took her prayer quite seriously!

Even before their graduation, Papa had already been going to Tõrva in the southeastern part of Estonia on weekends, and he and his brother, Oskar, had started leading church services and Bible studies with just a handful of believers. Soon a new congregation was established since there had been no evangelical church in the town. They elected Papa as their new pastor.

On December 1, 1925, Papa and Mamma were married in Tallinn at the Kalamaja Baptist Church. (This church still stands and is now called "Kalju Kirik" or the "Rock Church.")

In Tõrva, however, there was no church building so, with their little growing congregation, they soon started building their facilities. This took a lot of prayer and sweat. Many times the young married couple did not even have enough food to put on the table, as any money that the pastor received was put right back into the building of the church.

In the new church building, a small apartment was built upstairs for the pastor's family, where on August 8, 1929, Hulda Marie, and on December 5, 1930, Ester Elisabeth were born. The church was doing well, with great outreach to the community through Sunday school, youth work, choir, Bible studies, and of course, Sunday services. Many came to faith through this dedicated couple, who had sacrificed much by giving their all to building up His kingdom in this part of the country.

God, too, was faithful. Soon Papa received a call to become the assistant pastor of the largest evangelical church in Estonia. This was Mamma's home church in Ridala that had sent her to seminary. So in the fall of 1933 when Mamma was already expecting me, they bid their beloved Tõrva Baptist Church "good-bye" after nearly nine years of ministry and moved to Ridala. This is where I was born.

Chapter 3

Life in Ridala

I was five years old when we found out that we were going to have an addition to our family. Papa had been praying much for a son, and we girls were hoping for a little brother as well, although this time Mamma didn't set her hopes too high.

One day when Papa came home by train from Tallinn, the capital of Estonia a little over 100 kilometers northeast of Ridala, he brought us some special hard candy called lady fingers. They were about the length and width of a lady's small fingers and came in three colors—red, pink, and blue. Papa played a game with us before we could eat them. He would hide them in his closed hand and have us guess which hand had the candy. The sex of the baby to come would depend on the color we picked from his hand. Since both red and pink could be girls, there were always more chances that the baby would be a girl. But if we got the blue—of course we would all squeal with delight! We knew this was only a game and wouldn't make one bit of difference as far as a baby brother or sister was concerned, but it was fun to play and in the end we all got our candy.

As spring arrived, Mamma was getting bigger and bigger. On April 24, 1939, Papa took Mamma to the hospital in Haapsalu, nine kilometers away. We were so excited and could hardly wait for the big news. Finally, we learned that God had blessed our family with a baby boy! They named him Kaljo David Victor.

In those days, the mother and baby stayed in the hospital for a week, so we didn't get to see them right away, but what a special day it was when they arrived home! People came from all around to see them and one lady brought a beautiful cake with white whipped-cream frosting, decorated with fresh orange slices.

We couldn't keep our eyes off little Kaljo, though. He was such a sweet baby with soft blue eyes, blond hair, and a round face. As long as he kept sleeping or just lay there, both Hulda and I were happy watching him. But when it was time for a diaper change, Ester was usually the one who ended up doing it. I was too little and Hulda conveniently had other things to do.

With the arrival of spring, in order to get a really good start on their garden, Papa and Mamma always started by putting tomato, cucumber, radish, lettuce, and other seeds in boxes of good fertile soil and moving them from windowsill to windowsill to follow the sun during the day. The boxes had to be kept moist at all times and we girls got to help with that by watering. This was quite an art though, since too much water could drown the seeds and too little would dry them out. Our joy was great when little seedlings popped out their heads and soon grew to nice plants. These little plants had to be planted into bigger boxes and then taken to the hothouse that Papa had built for plants and flowers.

When it was warm enough and the soil had been prepared, it was time to replant them outside in the garden. The garden, or yard, was separated by a fence on our end of the church. We were allowed to use part of this yard where we also had some apple trees and berry bushes.

Since the land and area that the church had been built on was owned by the senior pastor, we were not allowed to eat from their fruit trees. He and his family lived across a rye field from the church, on a large farm. Their family came to pick apples and their sons threw the rotten apples at us if we happened to be outside. Still, throughout the summer, we not only had enough delicious vegetables and fruit to eat from our trees and bushes, but also for canning and making jam.

Papa also raised bees and had several beehives in the yard, so we always had fresh honey to eat and especially loved the times when he would come in the house carrying a honeycomb dripping on a plate. We gathered around the table with our spoons and he cut squares for us to chew on, spit out the wax, and savor the delicious honey. Mamma poured milk in our glasses and reminded us how blessed we were to live in the land of milk and honey. Sometimes we then sang a song about the "land flowing with milk and honey," like it says in the Bible: "*Kodumaa, Õnnis maa, Kus mett ja piima on, Kodumaa, Õnnis maa, Kus igavene rõõm ja õnn!*" We also used honey with sliced onion and hot tea to doctor our sore throats during wintertime.

Since Papa and Mamma loved flowers, they planted marigolds, asters, snapdragons, and many other types of flowers by the church front door and elsewhere in flowerbeds. These bloomed during the spring, summer, and fall seasons. One thing Papa always stressed was that we must clean all of the gardening tools after using them. To this day, as I put away gardening tools, I can never forget Papa's advice.

While Mamma was in seminary, then living in Tõrva and away from this part of the country, her half-brother Leo, when he was in his twenties, had left Estonia and settled in Argentina. Leo had a hard time finding work there in his field as an architect and instead, had become a whale hunter. In fact, he sent us a picture of himself taken while he was standing right on top of a huge whale. Leo married an attractive dark-haired Argentinean named Beba, and they had one daughter, Susanna, born in 1935. Susanna had blonde curly hair and when her mother walked around in the city of Buenos Aires with her, people would stop and admire this beautiful child. Although Mamma and the other relatives kept in touch with him through letters, we never got to meet Uncle Leo and his family.

However, Mamma's younger sister, Tädi (Aunt) Minda, along with her husband, Johannes Rõõmus, and family lived on a farm called Tale Talu located about two kilometers from us, so we visited with each other quite often. Because the soil in that area was much better than ours, we also had a garden plot there. It was kind of an outing for us to go to Tädi Minda's to weed and water the garden from time to time during the summer, since after the work was done we could play and run around with our cousins, blonde-haired Lehti and dark-haired Milvi, who were close to our age. They also had a younger brother, Arvi, and later a little sister, Evi, was born. Tale Talu was a large and prosperous farm with several horses, other farm animals, and many milking cows.

At home we had one cow, a sheep, and some chickens. In the spring a piglet was bought, and it would be butchered in the fall for meat. There was a barn for hay and for the animals.

While Papa was an assistant pastor for the first years in Ridala, no salary as such was allocated for him, but a plate was placed at the back of the church on the first Sunday of the month for a benevolent offering for whoever wished to put in any money for him. As a result, to really meet the needs of a growing family of six, the animals and produce were very necessary for our livelihood as well as to feed all of the guests who often stopped in or stayed for any length of time. This included visitors such as the guest speakers during the evangelistic meetings each winter and other visiting pastors and guests.

When school was out for summer vacation, our two cousins, Papa's sister Tädi (Aunt) Liisbet's daughters Astred and Daisy, nicknamed "Deps," usually came from Tallinn and stayed with us, bringing excitement and fun. Daisy was a year older than Hulda. She had nice wavy brown hair and was a lot of fun. Astred was very attractive, with beautiful blonde hair, and she was five years older than Daisy. She knew exactly what was "in" in the city. From her we learned what the latest styles and fashions were, what the popular songs were, and so on. She was also very artistic and showed us how to draw paper dolls and beautiful clothes for them.

God had given all of us girls artistic abilities, so we would draw and play with paper dolls for hours. We loved rainy days when we could play with our paper dolls, instead of doing outside chores. We grew very close to our cousins and it was a sad good-bye when they had to leave for the school year.

Tädi Minda marveled at how we girls got along so well and hardly ever fought or tattled on each other. If we did something that was not acceptable or hurt each other, we always had to ask for forgiveness, but that wasn't enough. We were then sent to our bedside where we were to kneel and ask God to forgive us and to make it right since we were told that we hurt Jesus by hurting our sister or brother. Then we would usually run back to the one we had wronged and exchange big hugs and kisses with each other.

Since Hulda and Ester were so close in age, they often did things together and then, understandably, I was left out. I was kind of a scaredy cat, afraid of spiders, bugs, and especially snakes. Hulda was the most outgoing and vocal one, but Ester was the bravest. She wasn't scared of the dark, and when it came to things like handling money or taking care of some errand, she usually did them. Both of my sisters had light brown hair that they braided when they grew older. Hulda's eyes are bluish-gray and Ester has grayish-green eyes.

Hulda's 7th birthday with cousins: Lehti, Daisy holding Mairy, Hulda, Ester; Back: Milvi, Astred, friend Asta

Since Hulda's birthday is in the summer (August 8), it was always celebrated with several cousins and sometimes with friends over. We played games outside, Mamma baked a birthday cake, and then our picture was taken together. Ester, Kaljo, and I don't remember any of our birthdays being celebrated, except on December fifth on Ester's birthday, Mamma would cut fir branches and put them in a big vase, which gave the house a "certain Christmas scent," thus bringing in the Christmas season on Ester's birthday.

Quite often, Papa went to Tallinn for church-related meetings, to buy something that was not available in Haapsalu, or to visit relatives. Now and then he took one of the children with him, and it was very special when I got to go along. We took a train from Haapsalu that made many stops at towns and hamlets during the ride that took nearly two hours. In Tallinn, we always stayed with Tädi Liisbet (Aunt Elisabet) and Onu Gutt (Uncle Gustav) and our cousins, Astred and Deps. They owned a little store right next to their apartment. I always enjoyed it when Tädi Liisbet let me go and "help" her and then give me candy.

The apartment building was owned by my Onu Aleksander, the eldest of Papa's brothers. The back side of the building also housed his soft-drink manufacturing facility. Onu Aleksander and his wife, Minna, lived on the second floor of the apartment house. By the time I visited my cousins in Tallinn, Helen, Aleksander's eldest daughter, whose mother had died along with Helen's twin sister during childbirth, had already immigrated to America. Aleksander and Minna had two daughters, Marta, who died at age twenty-one of an appendix attack, and Olga (Olli), who was married with two small children, Pilvi and Heikki.

Across the hall from my Tädi Liisbet's family lived Onu Oskar with his wife, Anni, and their family. Onu Oskar worked with his brother Aleksander in the soft-drink business, and he was also an evangelist. He was a gentle-spirited man who loved children. He would bend down and have me climb on his back and then have me slide down or else pick me up to sit on his lap and tell stories of when he and his siblings were young. Sometimes he also sang and taught us funny songs. Onu Oskar and Tädi Anni had four children. The eldest was Salme, who had also immigrated to America and was married with twin sons, Edward (Eddie) and Theodore (Teddy) Rukki. Onu Oskar and Tädi Anni's other children were Adele, Viktor, and Udo, who were all older than me. Some summers, Viktor and Udo visited us and they got a kick out of playing with their younger cousins and teasing us. One time Udo put on Papa's black baptismal robe and, with a scythe in hand, chased us all over the yard, crying out, "Death is coming! Death is coming! You'd better be ready!" We screamed and ran from him and finally all ended up laughing. So we got to see many of our relatives, both in Ridala and when we went to visit them in Tallinn. We became quite close to them as well.

In Tallinn, Papa took me to see some of the big city's twelfth- to seventeenth-century buildings and cathedrals, among them the pink Presidential Palace with its picturesque manicured gardens and sculptures, which left quite an impression on me. Once when I was in Tallinn, Tädi Liisbet gave me a shirt that had a tag on it in the shape of a bird. It seems that I was more impressed with the bird than the shirt. When Papa and I got home, I couldn't find the bird right away in the suitcase and kept saying, "I can't find my bird!" Everyone laughed at me when the bird finally turned out to be just a tag, instead of a toy bird!

Even though I remember so many happy days from my childhood, I must say that some days were not so good. I had blue eyes, freckles, and very fair, white skin, so sometimes my sisters called me "*lubjavanamees*," which means "whitewash man." I also had thin blonde hair. In fact my hair was so fine that Papa and Mamma decided that for it to grow and get thicker, it had to be cut off. Consequently, when I was about five or six years old, one day Papa cut off all my hair with clippers! I looked like a boy and didn't want people to see me. Most of the time I wore a little pink knitted hat with bows on either side and a ribbon tied under my chin to cover my bald head. Thank goodness, eventually hair does grow back, but I was very glad I wasn't going to school yet!

It was always a big occasion for us when a package from America arrived. Our Tädi Roosi (Papa's sister) with her husband August Kusik and their four grown children, John, Karl, Ella, and Erika, had immigrated to the US and lived in New York. Every now and then they sent us packages with some of their daughters' clothes. When I was quite young, they sent me a beautiful gray soft silk dress with a big parrot embroidered in front in all kinds of gorgeous colors (I'm

Mairy, age 6

wearing it in one of our Sunday school pictures). Another time they sent us a grown-up looking doll with long blue pants and a red jacket with a matching barrette. We called her "Prantsuse preili" or French Miss. Other times they sent us fashion magazines and between the pages we would find a pretty hanky.

Usually each fall and spring a friend who was a seamstress came to our house to sew clothes for us. The American clothes were then either re-sewn or altered to fit us or Mamma would buy several meters of fabric and we all got look-alike dresses. From my perspective, the sad part was that just when I grew out of my dresses, I still had two more identical hand-me-downs from Ester and Hulda to wear! One birthday, however, a nice lady from our church knitted a cornflower blue dress with pretty flowered buttons for me, which I remember vividly since no one else had a dress like mine!

Our Sunday School, 1937 (Mamma holding Mairy, middle of third row)

Mamma was the superintendent/teacher of our Sunday school, which was held upstairs above our apartment. We got Sunday school papers called "Little Stars" (Väiksed Tähed) and Mamma always ordered beautiful Bible story pictures from England. We had little "golden books" in which to place our stars after we had memorized our Bible verses. Besides many wonderful Estonian songs, she taught us to sing "Jesus loves me this I know, for the Bible tells me so . . ." in English. We also had other teachers, Tädi Tikas and

Tädi Hilda. (In Estonia, children address any grownup lady as "*tädi*," which means aunt, and a grownup man as "*onu*" or uncle, and add their first or last name. It is considered rude not to do so.)

The Sunday school performed for the big church on special occasions and on days like Mother's Day and Christmas. Once I got to lead the children's choir for Mother's Day, which I dearly loved to do, and some people then said that I would be the future choir director! The children learned Mother's Day poems and gave flowers to all of the mothers.

For Christmas there was always a huge tree in the sanctuary with tall live candles, held by wire candleholders with golden pinecones. We children marched to the wide platform to present our program of poems and songs. At the end of the service we received a little bag containing an apple, some hazelnuts, "*piparkoogid*" (Estonian gingerbread style cookies), a few wrapped candies, and a small Christian book. This brought us all great joy and excitement.

At home, Mamma kept a box of our Christmas tree ornaments on top of the wardrobe closet. We had some beautiful shining balls, birds with "silky" tails, and the candleholders for the white wax candles to attach to the tree. We also kept some of our homemade decorations, especially the little woven baskets that were a bit tricky to make out of shiny colored paper in this box, or made new ones to add to the collection. Usually we made new paper chains each year, as they often got crushed in the box. But it was always with anticipation that the decoration box was taken down. Then after carefully hanging each ornament, we all stood back in amazement to see the beautiful results.

At the beginning of summer break from Sunday school, we usually had our Sunday school picture taken and sometimes we went on an outing, which we looked forward to with great anticipation. The outing that stands out in my mind most was when I was about eight or nine and we took a big ferry to the island of Vormsi about fifteen kilometers off the coast of Haapsalu. Many Swedish-Estonians lived there and we went to visit another church. During most of the ferry trip we sang and when we got there, we sang and quoted scriptures and poems. After the church service we were invited to a big picnic that was set up outside on long tables.

I never knew my grandparents on Papa's side as they had both gone to be with the Lord by the time I was born, but my mother's parents lived about seven kilometers from us, so we saw them quite often. Our Vanaema (grandmother) was a talented weaver who made beautiful tablecloths and linens and wove colorful rugs and wall hangings on her loom from yarn she spun on her spinning wheel. The wool, of course, came from their sheep. She also knitted socks, multi-colored mittens in lovely designs, scarves, and hats for all her grandchildren as Christmas or birthday gifts. Vanaema also had a great talent for poetry and often composed the poems for our Sunday school children's programs. She loved the Lord and many of the themes she wrote about were about nature and God. Some of these were published, and one entitled "The Bible" even appeared in an Estonian Christian publication not long ago.

Our Vanaisa (grandfather) was a gentle man with a grayish curly beard. He was skilled in woodwork and made many things around the farm by hand. He read the Bible a lot, especially on long winter evenings after all the chores on their farm were done. Whenever he went to market in Haapsalu with first, his white and later, his brown horse and his buggy/sleigh, he usually stopped to see us on his way back, bringing us something that Vanaema had sent or that he had bought from the market in town.

The times that I especially remember going to our grandparents' farm was on February 23, which for both of them was their birthday. Usually Tädi Minda, with their family's horse and sleigh, picked Mamma and us children up and with our three cousins already on the sleigh, we headed for our grandparents' farm. Mamma and Tädi Minda always had some food with them and as we got there, we could already smell Vanaema's fresh birthday "*kringel*" being baked for the celebration.

We stayed overnight with Vanaema and Vanaisa. The kids all slept together in one big room. Once when I was still quite small, my "bed" turned out to be an empty old-fashioned bathtub with fancy legs. It was a very cozy place for me to sleep. After the evening prayers were said and all the lights were out, Vanaema stood by the big oven-wall to warm her back, singing a certain song that spoke of angels watching over the children *("Laste inglid alati Isa palet näevad nii")*. Everything was so peaceful and we knew that the angels were truly watching and keeping us safe.

Our grandparents gave Papa a motorcycle as a gift. Papa often made trips to our daughter churches, which were in the outlying areas. These churches were part of the big congregation but had their own services during the week and on most Sundays, although they came to our Ridala church for special occasions and sometimes on the first Sunday of the month when communion was celebrated.

Because I always wanted to go along with Papa on these visits, one day he said, "If you learn ten songs with all the verses, I will take you along and let you sing." That was no big challenge for me as I loved to sing and learned songs quickly—and my happy day came when I got to ride on the back of Papa's motorcycle on my first evangelistic tour and sing to my heart's content.

Every summer included different berry-picking times when most of our family took our pails and baskets and headed for the woods to pick blueberries, wild strawberries, lingonberries, or cranberries. In the fall season we picked all kinds of tasty mushrooms. However,

I will never forget one hot summer day when the picking for strawberries was extra good, but there were snakes also crawling around in the woods! This was very scary as some of them were poisonous. We could usually tell the poisonous ones by the zig-zag pattern on their backs; if we saw them we yelled out for Papa. He carried a long stick and always came to our "rescue" and killed them!

The old pastor, Tõnis Laas of the Ridala Baptist Church, was quite ill for a long time. When he died, Papa became the main pastor. Papa had already assumed the pastoral duties long before, and among other things he had started a youth group called "The Sunbeams" (*"Päikse Kiired"*). Many young people came to this group. The church had been growing under his ministry. Papa had a loving, shepherd's heart, and we often saw him before or after the church service going up to people, putting his hand on a person's arm, looking them in the eye and asking how they were doing. He had the gift of discernment to know when people were going through hard times or a personal struggle in their lives. He always counseled, encouraged, and prayed with them.

Every year revival meetings took place. People were baptized and new members were added to the church. We had a string orchestra for which Papa played the violin and Mamma the guitar. Later, when Hulda grew older, she played the mandolin and Ester the guitar. There was also a men's chorus, mixed choir, and the wind instrument group.

My Father's Guiding Hand

Each Sunday morning, long before the eleven o'clock church service began, people started coming early and began singing so heartily that the singing could be heard a long way off. Our church was known as the *"spirited and singing church."* Especially some of the older women praised God and clapped their hands or swayed together to the rhythm of the singing. There were Sundays when the Spirit of God was moving so powerfully that during prayer we felt and heard what seemed like a mighty rushing wind (palve kohin) sweep through the meeting. There were many prayer warriors in the congregation as well as older people who, though no longer able to make it to church, were still there through prayer and spirit.

Sometimes the services lasted for hours, as several preaching laymen gave shorter sermons. Papa would watch and see who among the brethren was sitting there with his finger between the pages of his Bible, looking to catch his attention. With his eyes and head, he pointed to them to be ready to share what God had reaveled to them during the week. As the pastor, he always prepared a sermon as well, but sometimes he preached to just tie up the loose ends. However, there seemed to be a spirit and a common thread and a theme prevailing throughout the services that only the Holy Spirit could orchestrate. Sometimes Papa also asked different ones to share ahead of time. Like I said, God had given my father an unusual gift of discernment to lead his flock in Ridala.

Life in Ridala

I should also mention the seating arrangement in the church. On one side of the platform were the "brethren," among them elders, in several rows. On one side of the sanctuary there were mostly women, children, and younger people toward the back. Across the aisle sat a mixture of people, and in the balcony, often and especially during the revival meetings, non-Christian teenage boys came to see what was happening. In school the next day, they whistled and hummed many of the new popular Christian songs they had heard.

During one such revival week, the evangelist (I believe his last name was Vardja), who stayed upstairs in our home, came running downstairs, singing, just after we had gotten into bed. The Lord had given him a new song with both words and melody that he wanted to share with us. He sat down at the harmonium and started joyfully singing (loose translation): "We're the hallelujah people of the Lord, and the people of His promise, yes we are, in the Holy Spirit's power praising Him, heading to our heav'ly home!"

Me üks halleluuja rahvas oleme,
Ja üks tõotatud rahvas oleme.
Püha Vaimu väes siin rõõmsalt hõiskame
Koju poole ruttame.

Meie juhiks Jeesus ise on meil ees
Usukilp ja vaimumõõk meil kõigil käes.

My Father's Guiding Hand

Arad, uskmatud ei seisa meie ees,
Kõiki võidame ta väes.

Pilgud lauldes ülespoole tõstame
Ilmakärast, vaevast läbi ruttame
Jumlat ja püharahvast näeme seal
Pea sinna jõuame! Halleluja!

This song had such a catchy tune and words that we all joined in and kept praising the Lord that night.

As the pastor's family, we were also the caretakers of the church. This meant that every week the big sanctuary had to be swept and the wooden pews dusted. We all helped, and then we three girls straightened out the pews, row by row. This had to be done just so—one would give instructions and the other two of us would move the pew an inch to the left or to the right to get them just perfectly lined up.

There was also lots of work outside for the whole family. The large churchyard was shaded on one side by huge willow trees and a picket fence, and the side facing the church by a high hedge of lilacs. Close to the lilacs, as well as toward the willow trees, were long hitching rails where each Sunday people who came with horse and buggy, or sleighs in the winter, tied their horses. We had to clean up after the horses. We girls also used the hitching rails as "balance-beams." We walked on them holding our hands wide apart, balancing ourselves to keep from falling. In fact, we learned to nearly run and do gymnastics and tricks on them.

Hitching rails alongside the church on a typical Sunday morning

During the fall there were lots of leaves to rake and in the winter plenty of snow to shovel. Now when I think back, I marvel at how my poor parents could manage all that, especially during blizzards when the wind had been howling all night and snow would sometimes be up to the waist by morning—to get everything shoveled and ready in time for Sunday morning services!

Baptisms usually took place on Pentecost Sunday. This meant that the huge baptismal tank that opened in the floor next to the platform needed to be filled. Many church volunteers came to help fill it from the outside well, bucket by bucket. We children each had our buckets, too, and joined in this busy time, carrying water up the incline across the yard, up the eight steps, through the hall, and into the tank. Then large birch branches with their fresh aroma were placed around the tank, standing up to give it a very solemn, festive look.

On the Sunday morning of the baptism, Papa and Mamma got up very early to heat water in a huge kettle on a woodburning stove in the cellar below the sanctuary. The water was then lifted up through a hole by buckets and added to the cold water to make it a little warmer. Luckily the tank had a plug in the bottom that was removed to empty it afterwards, letting the water flow outside through a hose and down the incline without more work!

Every year before Midsummer Day there was a whole-church workday when many volunteers came to clean the big sanctuary, including cleaning the tall windows. The long runners in the middle aisle were taken out and cleaned, and the entire wooden floor was scrubbed clean. Long tables and benches were set up outside the inner yard on the side of the church. Of course our family worked right alongside the others. Since Midsummer was the time of the Ridala Baptist Church's anniversary, there was always a big celebration that Sunday with lots of extra music and preachers who brought greetings from many other congregations. These services were very long, and afterwards everyone was invited to join in the fellowship and "love feast" at the tables set up outside. The ladies worked hard to prepare the food they had brought along, and whatever else was needed was fixed in our kitchen.

Besides other duties, my little job every Saturday afternoon was to clean the family's shoes and polish them to a brilliant shine. When the weather permitted, I usually polished them outside on the top ledge of our stone steps. Papa and Mamma saw to it that before sundown all work was completed and all of our clothes were clean and ironed for Sunday morning.

But as children we still had time for fun and games, too. Between the church building and the main road between Haapsalu and Lihula (called Lihula Highway) were several acres of rye fields owned by the old pastor's family and another farmer next to them. Between their fields was a foot/bicycle path to get straight to that main road from the church instead of having to go around the field by the gravel road that passed by the church gateway.

We often played in the rye field and picked bright blue cornflowers—the national flower of Estonia—and red poppies and white daisies. With this combination we could make beautiful head wreaths or put the flowers in a vase. We were not really supposed to be playing in the rye, but when it grew so tall, reaching over our heads, no one could see us there. So we played hide-n-go-seek along the narrow ditches that divided sections of the rye field. Once I lost Ester and Hulda and couldn't see either of them. I had lost all sense of direction and got really scared and started calling out to them, but they didn't answer me. I went on and on, turning back, then going in the opposite direction. Finally, almost crying, I thought that I should pray! So I got down on my knees and asked God to show me the right way to get back. As I hopelessly got up, I went straight ahead for some time, turned left . . . and there, right before me, was the foot/bicycle path! "Thank You, God! You always know the right way, but we need to admit our need and ask!"

Chapter 4

The Russians

In the fall of 1939, a drastic change occurred in our little free democratic country of Estonia. Germany had gone to war against Poland and the Western Allies (World War II began in September). The Russian government demanded military bases in Estonia. Since our own army was too small to fight a foreign occupation, we were forced to agree to let them set up their military bases. Unbeknownst to us, on August 23, 1939, the Molotov-Ribbentrop Pact had been signed in Moscow. The secret protocol of this pact decided the fate of the Estonian people for more than the next half a century since it impacted the people and lands that lay between the borders of Soviet Russia and Nazi Germany, subjecting them to brutal repression, murder, and genocide. We were victims of geopolitics.

After the Russians had set up their military bases in Estonia, they overthrew our government in June 1940, arrested our president, Konstantin Päts, and all the government leaders, sending them to Siberian prison camps. At that time, the Russians organized demonstrations where Russian civilians were brought in and, with a handful of Estonian communists and local bums, they demonstrated on our streets, demanding equal rights for the workers, calling, "Down with capitalist oppressors!" as well as demanding elections for a new government. Soon the so-called "new elections" took place where all eligible Estonians had to vote, but since there were only communist candidates, no matter whom you voted for, the communists ruled.

I will never forget the sad day when we watched through our bedroom window across the rye field toward the main road, as long columns of Russian troops marched in. They wore greenish uniforms and weird hats with pointed tops and sang communist songs that were mostly in the minor key. We soon learned that most of the communists' songs spoke of their "great country with all their power and might in their workers' paradise and how no one could conquer them with their mighty strength from Moscow."

After that, things really changed. Hulda and Ester told us what happened in their school and how new pictures appeared on the walls. Instead of pictures of Estonian leaders, now huge pictures of Stalin, Lenin,

Marx, and Engels peered down at the students. Because new textbooks could not be printed right away, the old ones were collected and pages that made reference to Christmas, the birth of Jesus, Easter, the Estonian flag, or patriotic expressions or freedoms were pasted together or the words were crossed out with black ink. Estonian history books were banned altogether. Instead, history soon was changed to tell about the great revolution in "our vast land of Russia," and how "our capitalism" had oppressed the working class, but now "all were equal."

There were immediately many far-reaching actions by the new Soviet masters. These eliminated individual liberties and civil rights and totally rearranged business life. All real estate, which included individual homes and farms as well as all commercial enterprises and rental properties, were confiscated from the owners and declared immediately to be part of the Soviet property. The owners received no compensation. Homeowners were allowed to stay in their homes but were allocated only very few square meters of floor space per person. The authorities determined how much floor area each family could have. If there was any "excess," other people, often strangers, were placed into homes and apartments to live in the "extra" space/room and to share the kitchen and bathroom. Russian officers with their families were brought to Estonia and later thousands of Russian people were brought to live and work in our land.

Similarly, the original farmers were allowed to keep a small portion of the land they owned but had to give most of their cattle, working horses, other farm animals, and farm equipment, etc., to the new communist authorities. They in turn distributed most of these to the "new" farmers as the powers decreed. No collective farms were formed at this time but were instituted in 1949 and later.

In our case, Papa's motorcycle was considered a "luxury," and it was taken from him. He had to resort to his old mode of transportation, the bicycle.

My thoughts go back to that first Christmas when we were under communist rule. There was to be no holiday on December twenty-fourth and twenty-fifth. No Christmas?!? We couldn't believe it! It was to be just another work and school day. In Estonia nearly everyone used to go to church on Christmas Eve, even those who didn't go during any other time of the year. That year especially, young people and children in cities and towns were being watched and, in some cases, patrols stood at the door and their names were written down if they dared to enter a church. We did have a quiet Christmas Eve service, but there was no children's Christmas program. That could jeopardize students' education, it was said. Later, Sunday schools and youth meetings were all banned.

As I did every year, I had memorized my Christmas poem. We always had a Christmas tree in the living room, but this year, no Christmas trees were sold anywhere. *Could we even have a tree?* we wondered. On December 24, Hulda and Ester came home from school while I helped Mamma at home bake and cook. Suddenly the door opened and in walked Papa with a tiny Christmas tree. Oh, how wonderful! We were having a tree after all! We all squealed with excitement and our baby brother Kaljo's eyes got big with joy. Papa said we had to keep quiet as we decorated the tree with pretty ornaments and made colorful paper chains. Mamma pulled down the shades and turned off the light as we gathered around the tiny tree. Quietly, we sang the familiar Christmas carols: "Silent Night, Holy Night" ("*Püha öö, õnnistud öö*"), "O come little children to Bethlehem" ("*Et tulge oh lapsed ja rutake nüüd Petlemma*"), "O Christmas Tree" ("*Oh jõulupuu, Oh jõulupuu*"), etc. We recited our poems and Papa read the beloved Christmas story from the Bible. Then we knelt around our tiny tree—the symbol of Christmas with its white live candles flickering and glowing in the dark room like the light of Jesus shining in the darkened world tonight. Suddenly I felt warm inside—such peace, joy—the love of Jesus. His presence was here. No communist rule could keep out the light of Christmas from our hearts. I prayed, "Thank You, Jesus for coming. Thank You, Jesus, for loving me. Thank You, Jesus, for our tiny Christmas tree!"

We opened our presents and were once again so happy to receive new mittens with pretty designs on them. We went around the room, hugging and kissing each other with the joy of Jesus in our hearts. Then we all had some delicious Christmas foods: barley sausage with lingonberry sauce, headcheese, pork roast, oven-browned potatoes and sauerkraut, candied pumpkins, etc., and for dessert, fruit compote, sweet raisin bread, and of course some "*piparkoogid*" (gingerbread cookies), which are a traditional part of all Estonian Christmases.

The winter of 1940 was very cold and it seemed that the fierce east winds and snow blew in from the depths of Russia, bringing even wolves and wild boars with it. Everything seemed so gloomy. Papa had to write out his sermons each week and submit them to the NKVD (later called the KGB) before he could preach on Sunday mornings. One never knew when a spy would sit in the congregation to check that Papa followed his text.

One day after the war between Germany and Russia had broken out and he was at the NKVD headquarters again, Papa was told that they needed his services during the week at the Haapsalu hospital. Since the war continued, many wounded soldiers were being brought to Estonian hospitals for treatment. With Papa's medical background and a practicing license in medicine, his skills were now needed there. Papa told us that as the wounded soldiers were brought in from the battlefield, their uniforms and underwear were full of lice and fleas. In order to wash them, they were put into a huge kettle to boil. The grease from the little insects was so thick on top of the water that it had to be removed with a big ladle before any soap would even get them halfway clean. With his fluent Russian and compassionate heart, Papa ministered to and encouraged these soldiers, even though, under the watchful eyes of the authorities, this could be dangerous.

Later, Papa was transferred to a hamlet called Kullamaa to work in a clinic where Estonian young men had to be given physical examinations before being conscripted into the Russian army. Our fun-loving nineteen-year-old cousin Udo from Tallinn, who had just been admitted to the university with high honors, had already been sent to Russia to fight in the Red Army. We never heard from him again.

When Papa did the physicals, he "freed" several young men from military duty who he knew had small children or a sick mother or expectant wife at home, by writing on their documents that they had some kind of illness or disease. Some other men, however, resorted to hiding in the woods to escape military duty. Papa was seldom able to come home and preach on Sundays, but when he did he had to be back by Monday morning in Kullamaa.

Several times the Russians came to search our home. The first time they took away our radio, telephone, even a big city map of Tallinn that we had upstairs on a wall. Often they didn't even know how to open certain closets or Mamma's purse, so they either broke them or used their rifle to shoot things open. In the attic Mamma kept a trunk full of homemade soap and without realizing it, she had locked it and couldn't find the key at the moment when a soldier demanded that she open it. Of course, he wouldn't believe her that it only contained soap—so, bang! went his rifle, followed by his sheepish look when he saw what was inside.

One time, Papa and Mamma were both home and two NKVD officers who came asked them a lot of questions, wanting to get information about our church members. At one point, one of the officers looked at us girls and said, "These girls have already been poisoned by the capitalist ideas." Then, picking up our little brother, he said, "Now this young man will grow up to be a real Stalin's boy." Of course they were hoping to brainwash him at such a young age with all the dogma of communism.

Another time when Mamma had gone to help Vanaema and Vanaisa make hay and we were playing outside with our cousin Deps from Tallinn, a car came into our yard. Ester and I ran into the bushes to hide, but Hulda and Deps faced the two officers head on. They actually started flirting with the girls, but since the girls had already learned some Russian in school, they answered back firmly that they wanted no part in this! Finally the men left and Ester and I sighed a breath of relief.

The Russians

This was actually a very hard time for us with Papa being gone from home so much. We heard of more and more people being arrested all over Estonia. Usually the arrests were made during the night. Only a few minutes were given to get dressed before being loaded into a truck at gunpoint and taken to the nearest railroad station for deportation to Siberia. A horrible fear settled over the land! One never knew when that fateful knock would come to one's door. We found out that our cousin Olli (from Tallinn) and her husband, Osvald, had been arrested and sent to different Siberian slave camps. (Many years later, we found out that they both died there). Osvald was part of the former Estonian military personnel and Olli had been an active Girl Scout leader. Their young children, Heikki and Pilvi, were spared only because they had been spending the summer on their grandparents' farm in Kernu that Onu Aleksander and Tädi Minna had bought and moved to before the communist takeover.

As a precaution because of this constant fear, we would either get dressed and then put our nighties on top at night, or else we would have our warm clothes nearby and a travel bag ready. But oh, how I praise God for our faithful parents! Instead of shaking and worrying, they said, "This is the perfect time to learn Scripture verses!" (The summer nights in Estonia are light enough so one can quite easily read a good-size print.) We knew that if we were sent to a slave camp, we wouldn't have a Bible.

We needed God's Word to give us spiritual strength. We knew, too, that there would be thousands of others who would be without hope, and we could share His Word to comfort them and give them the words of life. We had learned the Twenty-third Psalm and other Bible verses that gave us assurance that God would be with us, but it was then that we also memorized the ninety-first Psalm, which became so important to us:

> He who dwells in the shelter of the Most High Will abide in the shadow of the Almighty. I will say to the Lord, "My refuge and my fortress, My God, in whom I trust!" For it is He who delivers you from the snare of the trapper, And from the deadly pestilence. He will cover you with His feathers, And under His wings you may seek refuge; His faithfulness is a shield and bulwark. You will not be afraid for the terror by night, Or of the arrow that flies by day; Or of the pestilence that stalks in darkness, Or of the destruction that lays waste at noon. A thousand may fall at your side, And ten thousand at your right hand; But it shall not approach you... For He shall give His angels charge concerning you, to guard you in all your ways. They will bear you up in their hands, lest you strike your foot against a stone... He will call upon Me, and I will answer him; I will be with him in trouble; I will rescue him and honor him. With a long life I will satisfy him, and let him know My salvation. (NASB)

The Russians

Wow! What assurance to know that no matter where I would be, no matter what would happen to me, my GOD would be with me! He *shall* send His angels to watch over me! One night as we were reciting these Bible verses, we heard a truck stop by our church/home. Out jumped several Russian soldiers, who surrounded the building. Two solders with pointed rifles rushed up our steps and banged on our door! We gasped, "Oh, God, is this it?!" Mamma walked to the door to open it as the men marched in and one said, "We are checking this house," and without another word started searching all our rooms. They looked in the closets, under our beds, through the sanctuary—all over. Then one officer said, "That is all," and they left as suddenly as they had come. We in turn fell to our knees and thanked God that we had been spared this time. We presumed that perhaps they were looking for young Estonian men referred to as "brethren of the forest," who would be in hiding to avoid being taken to the Russian Army.

The night of June 14, 1941, will never be forgotten in the heart and mind of every Estonian, and to this day it is commemorated as a day of mourning. That night, over 15,000 men, women, and children were arrested, hauled onto trucks and then cattle cars at the nearest railroad station that eventually formed into trains in Tallinn or Tartu to head east . . .

The night of March 16, 1949 (after we had left Estonia), was another mass deportation when over

22,000 were taken the same way, in addition to the thousands of others taken at different times, individually or in smaller groups. Most of them perished without graves. Many died in the cattle cars from lack of food or disease that broke out somewhere in the deepest forests or plains on their way to Siberia and were then just thrown out into the woods for wild animals to eat. Others died in slave camps under hard labor, cruel beatings, cold, or starvation. Their bodies were dumped into mass graves or during winter, before the ground froze, bulldozers would dig a big hole in the ground and then, throughout the winter, as people died, they were thrown in. When spring came once again, the bulldozers returned to cover the dead bodies with dirt.

Usually there was no reason given for the arrests or if it was given, it was absurd or senseless and there was no legal recourse to protest. Those arrested were usually businessmen, politicians, government workers, teachers, leaders in any given field, pastors, and Christians with various occupations. Many had owned their homes or farms, but all were labeled as "capitalists," and therefore, even children were enemies of the state—the new regime.

As Estonians continued to live in fear of who might be arrested next, the warfront drew closer to Estonia and to the part of the country where we lived. One day as Ester and I were out in the pasture tending a few sheep, we saw a Russian plane flying overhead so low that we could feel the impact of the wind and clearly see the red five-cornered stars on its wings. Because the sheep ran in every direction, we had quite a time getting them calmed down to graze again.

A few evenings later when Papa was in Kullamaa again and Mamma was making pancakes, we heard machine gunfire. We ran down to our cellar below ground. Mamma grabbed the plateful of pancakes and followed us. As evening turned to night, we stayed there holding our breath each time we heard more artillery shooting, followed a few seconds later by explosions. We thanked God when there was a break in the firing. Mamma started singing quietly. We all joined her in a beloved hymn, "When my Jesus Christ will lead me, Then no harm to me will come, But without Him I'd be wandering, Through this land below alone." ("*Oh kui mind mu Jeesus saadab, Ei siis kahju karda ma, Aga üksi ma ei julgeks, Ilmast läbi kõndida*"); "The Lord's our Rock in Him we hide, a shelter in the time of storm . . ." ("*Me Jumal on üks varjupaik, mis tormi ajal seisma jääb . . .*"); and many other songs that talk about our God's protective hand.

Finally toward the wee hours of the morning, the shooting ceased. Quietly, we left the cellar and peeked out. Everything was so still! The sun was rising. Suddenly the birds started singing. A new day was dawning. The Russians had backed off and were losing the battle to the Germans, retreating with their war front back towards their own country. Were we free?!

We ran outside to look around. We saw empty bullet shells, but not one had hit our building. It was truly like God had "sent His angels to watch over us – to guard us in all our ways," as the Bible says in Psalm 91:11.

Chapter 5

New Occupation

We were so relieved! It was August 1941 and we could tell that the Russians had truly left our country as the German troops marched in. Looking up the road, we saw German soldiers in open army trucks and tanks moving along. People ran out to meet them and greet them with flowers. Were these our new liberators who came to us with new hope? Anything and anyone would be better than the terrorist boot of Stalin and the Red regime!

Things in our life took a new turn. Papa was able to return home and resume his pastorate on a regular basis. Church was no longer a forbidden place to go. All church activities and programs were back to normal and with a grateful heart to God, we could again worship Him freely.

Soon Papa had to go to the county courthouse to get some papers. There, to his dismay, the new Estonian clerk showed him a list of names that was left behind by the Russians when they retreated in a hurry. Among this list were the names of: Peter Viktor Konsa, Adele, Hulda, Ester, Mairy, and Kaljo Konsa . . . to be arrested and deported to certain destinations in Siberia on the *very night* that we were in our cellar as the Germans and Russians were fighting in our area. It was almost too hard to believe that truly, once again, God had sent His angels through the German troops to watch over us in perfect timing!

To most of the Estonian people, since we were of the Aryan race, the Germans and the Nazi government were friendly as long as one was not a Jew.[3]

When one section of an army battalion was moving through the area, they needed extra housing and so were housed in our church building for a week, moving out before Sunday. They were courteous, clean, and well-mannered. They gave us chocolates and told us they missed their families back home. Among them Papa and Mamma found some Christians and invited them to have devotions with us. We sang hymns in German and read the Bible and prayed together. Tears came to their eyes as they expressed their joy of being in a Christian family, which they had missed since being in the army, fighting in a foreign land. Besides conquering Estonia and the other two Baltic States, Latvia and Lithuania, the German troops were marching ahead and conquering large parts of Russia.

Many Estonians, who had remained living in Russia after Papa's family had immigrated back to Estonia during the Czarist rule, had been living under very hard circumstances. Under Stalin's communist regime, they were being sent to hard labor camps and many were outright killed during the purges in 1937-38. The Germans allowed those Estonians who were still in their homes to move back to Estonia.

When Papa heard that there was a trainload of these Estonians being brought to Haapsalu, he went to the railroad station where these people were standing and waiting for someone to perhaps claim them as relatives or take them home to help as farmhands or domestics, or to offer some other work and a place to live. As people mingled with each other, one of our relatives later told us what he was thinking. His name was Voldemar (Volli) Konsa, and he was fourteen at the time. He had come to Estonia with his Christian grandmother, their goat, and a few belongings. When he had seen a very kind-looking gentleman walking among the people, he had thought, *Oh, I hope this kind man will come and take us home with him.*

Suddenly he heard that man say, "Are there any Konsas here?" His ears perked up and he called out, "I'm a Konsa! Please take me!" Of course, Papa brought Volli, his grandmother, and their goat home with him.

The goat stayed in our barn. We all went out to pet her and after milking, tasted her milk, which was somewhat different from our cow's milk.

It was good to meet these relatives about whom until now, we had known nothing. Our hearts went out to them as Grandmother Emilie (Miili for short) told us of how their farm near Pohki had been taken away from them and her husband, Mihkel Konsa, was sent to the Gulag for ten years where he died near the Mongolian border. Their son Konstatin and his wife, Maria, (Volli's parents), had both been arrested under Stalin's "purging" in 1937 and then killed at the age of thirty-two in St. Petersburg (renamed Leningrad by that time) prison. Volli had come to live with his grandmother when his parents got work in Leningrad and stayed with her when they were arrested. Grandmother Miili further shared about their other relatives and the separations, hardships, and killings under the communist rule. (Much later we learned that out of about 6,000 Estonians who had lived in Russia, only fewer than 300 were still left after the 1937-38 purging.)

Christmas came and Mamma also gave Volli a Christmas poem to memorize for Sunday school which he, along with the other children, performed that Christmas Eve. The poem talked about the wise men looking for the star (Targad vaatvad, targad vaatvad, vaatvad tähti "taiva" all . . .). We girls giggled; we thought it sounded so cute and funny at the same time how he pronounced his words, especially the word "taeva" since they spoke Estonian with a kind of funny Russian or partly the old Tartu—the origin of Papa's heritage—accent, but of course we understood them fine.

A month or so later, our Onu Aleksander, who now with his wife, Minna, lived on a large beautiful farm by a lake at Kernu some distance from us (where our cousin Olli's children were also living by then) took them in as they actually did have household work and needed some help on their farm.

Because Papa had not been feeling well and sometimes had great pain in his stomach, he went to the Haapsalu Hospital for some tests and found out that he had stomach ulcers. Soon after that he had to have an operation where two-thirds of his stomach was removed. Being the doctor that he was, he brought the affected part of his stomach home in some yellowish liquid in a glass jar! (We were glad that he didn't just display it on his dresser!) After that, he had to eat smaller portions, eat more often, and be somewhat careful as to what he ate. He could no longer do much heavy labor, but he continued to be the pastor and still did the gardening and so on.

Chapter 6

My School Days

The new school year began. The law in Estonia at that time was that a child should start school either at age seven if her birthday was in the same calendar year as the start of the school year, or at eight. So in the fall when I started school (under the German occupation) I was eight years old, but since my birthday comes in January, I already turned nine before I finished the first grade. However, usually parents or older siblings taught the younger ones the basics of reading, writing, and arithmetic by the time they entered school.

I had eagerly looked forward to going to school and, together with Hulda and Ester, now I was finally able to go. The road to *Parila Algkool* (Parila Grade School) from our house was three kilometers. It was fine to walk this distance when the weather was nice, but in pouring rain or deep snow, it was something else. There were also other children from the neighborhood who joined us along the road to school. It seems like we always had various adventures on the way or else, if nothing exciting was happening, Hulda thought of something fun to do (she is the "idea generator" in our family with new fantasies in any situation).

Sometimes on our way home from school we would stop at the two cemeteries to look at all the different gravestones. The boys tried to scare the girls by telling ghost stories related to graveyards. Other times, if there was a funeral going on, we would go to see who was being buried or whether we knew the person, or just to listen to the singing or sermon and see how many flowers were brought. The more flowers there were, it meant that the person had many friends and relatives, was well liked, or was someone of importance. Sometimes, on nice spring days before going home, we went to pick flowers on Tubrimäele, a nearby hill, where we knew there were lots of blue anemones (*sinililled*) or we picked daisies along the roadside and wove head-wreaths for our mothers.

One winter morning as we were walking toward Parila in deep snow and hoping for a horse and sleigh to come along, we finally saw one coming behind us. As it approached us, Hulda yelled out and asked if we could hitch a ride with the farmer sitting in front of his load of grain sacks, heading for the Parila flour mill.

The man very rudely snapped back, "NO," and cracked his whip at the horse. But just as quickly, we jumped on the back of the sleigh runners and hung on tightly to the back railing of the open sleigh. The man behind his sacks had no idea that we were getting a ride until suddenly he cracked his whip again. The sleigh jerked, the railing broke off, and we three landed flat on our backs on the snowy road with the broken railing in our hands! I guess he found out when he got to the flour mill that "someone" had taken off with his sleigh railing!

All of the farmers were not as mean as that one. Coming home from school once, a farmer was heading to the meat market in Haapsalu with his great big butchered pig on his open sleigh. He was sitting on top of the pig's nose and when we asked for a ride, he said to just climb on top or on either side of the pig and ride along! Although there was a blanket covering the pig, we still kept sliding off its back as everyone was laughing so hard, and the farmer also joined in on our fun.

The schoolhouse had double doors leading to a fairly large hall with benches along the walls and hooks above them for hanging our coats. We ate sandwiches that we had brought from home and during cold weather exercised and played games here. This room was also used for any assemblies after opening folding doors to our classroom of three primary grades, where my teacher, Mrs. Anni Säin, taught.

The school principal, Mr. Arvo Raatma, taught the upper three grades and he and his wife lived in a small apartment right at the schoolhouse. If hot water was needed for coffee or tea for any function, it was heated on the principal's wood-burning stove in their kitchen. There was no plumbing in the building; instead there was an outhouse with one side for boys and the other for girls. Big wood-burning stoves in the various areas heated the school.

I liked going to school and being with other kids. My favorite subjects were art, penmanship, and writing, but my very favorite was music. We learned and memorized many songs that talked about nature, the beautiful springtime, flowers, and birds, but also many Estonian patriotic songs about loving our country and our blue, black, and white flag. All these songs and also many poems learned in school, Hulda, Ester, and I can still sing and recite.

Once a week there was a class called "Religion" ("*Usuõpetus*"), as Estonia was predominately Lutheran. Here the Ten Commandments, the Lord's Prayer, and some basic Christian teachings were taught. During recess and after eating lunch, we played "ring games" ("*ringmängud*"). There are many such games in Estonia, and some resemble "Ring around the Rosie," but much more sophisticated and with lots of actions and variations. Others are more like folk dances accompanied by singing.

When the weather was nice, we played outside in the three different play areas. Games went on for bigger and smaller students. There was soccer, volleyball, or one called "*laptuu*," which is something like baseball, as well as games like "Last couple out," ("*viimane paar tagant välja*") "Fish into sea" ("*kiisad merre*"), "Wolf and hunter" ("*hunt ja jahimees*"), and "Egg" ("*muna*"), with plenty of running and yelling to accompany the action.

During the summer, as mentioned before, we enjoyed playing with our cousins Lehti and Milvi. One time when we had been weeding and watering our garden plot at Tädi Minda's farm and the work was done, we started playing with our cousins inside. Later, when everyone ran out again by way of their cement-floor entryway, I slipped and fell flat on my face. My mouth was bleeding and my permanent front tooth was cut in half! It took some time for the bleeding to stop and more time for the scar to heal, but the permanent half-tooth that I now had in my mouth stayed that way for several years to come. So whenever I laughed or was in any picture, I always tried to smile with my mouth closed.

But at home or at nighttime, my half tooth did not stop me from laughing. I often laughed when I had the treat of sleeping with Hulda and Ester in their wide "golden" bed. Hulda always thought of some neat stories or fantasies. One time she started telling us a make-believe story she called "The Adventures of the Mouse Family." Actually, I was really scared of real mice, but when Hulda told the "mouse stories," these creatures were so cute and cuddly. She told us how they lived between the wall, how they got little bits of clothing, like a piece of red velvet, and how the mommy mouse made tiny chair cushions from that, how they acquired special cheese, played mouse-games, or went to mouse school. These were continuous stories and could go on and on, night after night. Ester and I would add some little part of the story to try to make it even more interesting. So to this day, it is just our "sisters' thing" – when we see some cute little mouse picture in a magazine or a card, we cut it out and share it with each other. This may seem very silly to others, but there are so many such little things that we three sisters share. We say a certain word that has "our own special meaning," a certain song that Papa sang or taught us, or a certain way Mamma did something. One of us says some word that triggers off a particular phrase in a song – and the other two start singing a related song. It is so uniting, and a "feeling" and a "knowledge" that can never be shared or even fully explained to anyone else. I imagine that someone who has really special sisters like I have can in some way identify with this.

In 1943, as in previous years during evangelistic meetings, people came to the Lord, among them many youth, including Hulda and Ester. When the invitation was given and people went forward, they knelt down and usually prayed with a counselor, but if they did not really receive the assurance of salvation, they would come back the next night and pray again until they were sure that the Holy Spirit filled them. It wasn't just that one made a decision to receive Christ and was called a Christian. There was a "new birth" that actually took place. Consequently, there were very few people who walked away from the Lord or were backslidden.

That year, Pentecost Sunday was a special day in our family when Papa baptized many young people, as well as some adults, among them his two older daughters. Hulda was thirteen and Ester was twelve at the time.

In September when school began again, Hulda started high school in Haapsalu while Ester and I continued at the grade school in Parila. During my second grade year, a friend from our church, Robert, made me an orange-colored pair of wooden cross-country skis for Christmas. What a wonderful gift! I learned to ski quite well and enjoyed my time of gliding over the snow. Sometimes the weather got so cold and the snow so hard that Papa could actually ride his bicycle on top of the snow. When it got to -20 degrees Celsius (-4F), schools were closed and we could then stay home.

Someone gave us the cutest puppy dog. He was medium brown with a pure white front and paws and, because he looked like a little ball of cotton, we named him Vati (meaning cotton). Even when Vati grew older, he remained small in stature. It was even more fun to watch him when we took him outside to play in the snow. When the snow got deep, he would almost get lost in it and bark so we could go find him. He became such a part of our family as he followed us all around.

There was a long picket fence by the edge of the church property right next to a row of tall willow trees. At times, snowdrifts piled up high against the fence in such a way that on one side of it we could dig tunnels and cut big "bricks" to build igloos and enjoy playing house. Vati joined right in with our fun and games. When the snow was wetter, we made snowmen and had snowball fights.

The "kick sled" as it is called in English (*soomekelk*), was something else that brought us great enjoyment. These sleds are like a chair with two metal runners on the back on which one or even two people can stand, hold on to the handlebars on the back of the "chair," and push (or kick) with one foot. When one gets enough speed or goes downhill, one can put both feet on the runners (in a way, like on a scooter), and another person can sit on the seat, or it can be used to hold bags or packages. Across the road from us, toward the coast, was a wide swampy meadow. When it was frozen over and fresh snow had fallen, we took the "kick sled" and made paths to glide along. We had a great time with Hulda and Ester standing and pushing on the runners, me sitting and holding Kaljo on my lap, and Vati running and barking behind us.

This was still wartime. As the conflict between Russia and Germany escalated, more and more Estonian young men were conscripted into, now, the German Army or Air Force. Stores were fairly empty and food was increasingly scarce, especially in cities, and it was mostly rationed. Farmers had to now, as before for Russians, deliver food to fulfill quotas required by the Germans.

Usually on our way home from school we would stop at one of the two stores in Ridala to see what could be bought. During the Russian occupation, the Russians had emptied all our stores, since they had never seen such abundance like we had in Estonia when they confiscated all of our businesses. Ester had, in fact, been able to buy the very last pair of shoes in a store in Haapsalu for the new school year before the Russians retreated.

Now besides foodstuff, about the only things available in stores were matches and pencils. We picked up our mail at the bigger of the two stores where the mailboxes were lined up on one side of the wall. Our mailbox number was 9 (the address was Parila p.k. 9, Haapsalu). During these war years, all mail was censored and we were never able to receive letters from our relatives overseas nor write to them.

Once when Papa came back from a visit to Tallinn, he had somehow managed to buy an orange, a rarity during wartime, from some store or market. He made a "big occasion" out of it by gathering all of us around him. He then took out his pocketknife, which was a special knife that Papa had had since he lived in Germany. He had told us that his knife could "speak German." He opened up the blade, held it up, and then let the blade slowly drop down, at which time it made a slight noise going "tick-tick-tick."

On this occasion, he said, "Children, you know where oranges are grown? In different countries where the climate is warm and they never have real cold winters or snow, like in the tropics." He went on, "But this particular orange is grown in Palestine [from an area which later became]—Israel. Remember who came from Israel?"

We all shouted, "Jesus! Wow!" and excitedly I asked, "Really, from the same land where Jesus was born, where He lived and walked?"

Papa went on. "Yes," and then added, "We don't just gobble down a delicacy like an orange, but we must also eat it with our "mind" and visualize this whole thing."

Then he used his "smart German knife" to cut the skin of the orange into equal sections, peeling the skin back like a lotus-bloom. After that, he opened up the orange the same way, sectioning it like an open flower-bloom.

"Oh! How beautiful!" We all watched in amazement. Then came the best part! We each got a piece and slowly bit into the juicy fruit, thinking and savoring the taste . . . yum, yum. Oh, how rich we were to learn and appreciate all these special things that our Papa made us aware of and taught us.

Estonia's National Independence Day, February 24, 1944, stands out in my mind. It was the last time the Estonian people were able to celebrate the day openly until 1992. During the Russian occupation, one could be sentenced to jail or concentration camp for several years for simply flying the beautiful blue-black-white flag. However, on that cold and snowy day in 1944, despite the German occupation, all the homes and streets again were lined with Estonian flags. Papa, Ester, and I had come to Haapsalu and went with Hulda to her high school auditorium, which was filled to capacity with people. There was a formal Independence Day program with an orchestra, choirs, and speeches.

When we came out after the program, we saw a mass of people gathering as a parade was forming with brass bands, people carrying Estonian flags, and soldiers marching in German uniforms. We recognized several of the young soldiers from our church and community. Everyone joined the parade and soon we reached the market square where wreaths were placed by the Monument to the Fallen Soldiers. At the closing, the band played "Nearer my God to Thee" ("*Ligemal Jumal sul*"). The soldiers were to leave the next day in special Estonian battalions to fight against the Red Army. Of course, we cheered them on to victory!

Because of the blackouts, quite often at night we couldn't turn on the electricity. With the help of a couple of friends, Papa had installed our electricity, which was run by wind turbine and could light the whole building. But when lights had to be out and we needed to do our homework in the evenings, we studied by oil lamps with glass cover shades. The glass had to be cleaned each night as black soot gathered on them. We also had a tiny oil lamp called "tattnina" or so-called "snot nose," since, if anyone sneezed or blew their nose, the little flickering light would blow out.

As the winter wore on, bomb raids took place more often with Russian planes hitting our cities and towns. People had to run to shelters, often spending nights there. On March 9, 1944, the biggest bomb raid took place in Tallinn when large sections of our capital city and surrounding areas were destroyed, and many people were killed or wounded.

This, of course, interrupted the lives of many. People from cities were trying to move to safer places, and some came to the country with some of their belongings to trade for food with the farmers. The school year was cut short. Hulda, who was boarding with a relative while going to high school in Haapsalu, came home. Our cousin Astred from Tallinn lived with us some of the time and several other families stayed now and then. Since our grade school stayed open, Ester and I were able to finish the school year.

Siblings, Summer 1944, Ridala. Ester, Mairy, Kaljo, Hulda holding Vati

As summer turned into early fall, the Russians were pushing back the Germans, and the war front was moving closer and closer to Estonia. Friends and relatives were quietly talking among themselves about trying to escape before the Russians again captured our land. Many did escape by boats to Sweden or with the retreating Germans by land or ships to Germany. We, however, had no way of escaping and sensed that most likely we would be among the first to be deported to Siberia. We had already been on that "black wanted list," since Papa was a Baptist minister and had "committed a big crime" by excusing some of the Estonian young men from being taken into the Red Army.

Meanwhile, Papa continued to work as the pastor and made his usual house calls, often visiting the shut-ins and the sick. On one such visit, after reading the Bible and praying by the bedside of a Christian brother, the man asked Papa, his pastor, to go to his dresser and open the bottom drawer where he told Papa to take out a little box. When Papa opened it, he found gold coins in it!

Then the man said, "Pastor, God has placed it on my heart to give this to you. Do not use it for any of the Lord's work here. This is for you and your family. God will show you what you will need it for."

Papa was very amazed, surprised, and grateful and of course thanked this brother, brought it home, and put it in his bottom dresser drawer.

A short time later, Tädi Maria Tikas, a close friend and a Sunday school teacher at our church, came to see us and quietly talked with Papa and Mamma about someone who had a boat for sale. She said, however, that the only commodity that he would accept for payment was gold or silver. "And who has that much gold or silver?!" she added.

Before Papa said anything else, he bowed his head and said, "Thank You, Father, all gold and silver is Yours, and You know what Your children need, even before we ask!"

After some more discussion and prayer, he took the "gift from God" and went with Tädi Tikas to see the boat owner in Haapsalu. After bargaining with this man, he would not come down on his price, saying, "Take it or leave it."

Papa had counted the gold at home, and it was *exactly* the amount of gold coins he had been given! God, You truly know what and how much Your children need!

Chapter 7

Our Escape

Papa and Mamma had told us that it was necessary to leave Estonia and perhaps go to Sweden for a time as the Russians had already re-occupied a large part of our land. Emotionally, this was very difficult for our parents, especially for Papa to leave his beloved flock. He prayed and battled with the Lord about it.

On September 22, our brother, Kaljo, was very sick with some kind of flu and a fever. That evening we all knelt by his bed as Papa prayed, "Lord, show us Your way. What are we to do? If it truly is your will that we leave everything here, show us by healing Kaljo."

Very early the next morning, September 23, 1944, as Mamma woke us up, Kaljo was already awake and running around joyfully! By faith, Papa and Mamma had been up most of the night making preparations for leaving. It was still half dark when Mr. Tikas's car pulled up, and we children had to leave for the coast where our boat was. The quick sad hugs and good-byes to our little brown dog, Vati, our Tädi Anni, and others, were tearful. The last look around our home and all that was dear to me since my birth was painful. Yet we hoped that this was temporary and soon the Russians would be driven out of Estonia with the help of the British or Americans and we could return. But that was not to be, because actually they were fighting on the same side as the Russians.

The drive, with a few of our belongings, took us about ten minutes on the country road to Tikas's summer place in Topu by the sea. It was a sunny autumn day as we waited for Papa, Mamma, and the others to arrive. We saw some Russian planes overhead and heard bombing. We ran for cover into the barn. Later we found out that the Rohuküla harbor near Haapsalu had been bombed.

Meanwhile, our Aunt Anni, who had stayed with us, had started walking toward Haapsalu but then stopped by the roadside to kneel and pray in the woods that her son would make it here on time before our boat left. After praying, she continued to walk, and suddenly she saw her twenty-six-year-year-old son Viktor, whom she had prayed for, running toward her with a briefcase in hand. He had barely caught the last train from Tallinn to Haapsalu. The two of them hugged and kissed each other good-bye and, with his mother's prayer and blessings,

Our Escape

Viktor continued running toward Ridala to reach us before we left with the boat.

Finally we saw everyone arriving with their bags. In order to fit everyone into the boat, most of the baggage had to be re-packed and some left behind for lack of space. After our farewell prayer, we got into a little rowboat, a few at a time. This boat took us some meters from the shore to where our motorboat was anchored.

A local fisherman, Mr. Rannus, was to be our captain, and his wife was also along. Jaan Pottsep, an engineer, with his wife, Milvi, (friends of the Tikas) became the motorist and besides them, the other passengers were: Jüri and Maria Tikas and Aleksander Reins (good family friends); cousin Viktor Konsa, and our family of six, making it fourteen people altogether.

Some days earlier our boat had been brought to the Topu coast from its previous location about five kilometers to the south when the threat that the Russians were coming back became serious. This was done secretly during the night by two dear Christian brethren, Aleksander and August Krabi. The boat was placed on a cart, pulled by their two horses, and quietly moved through the woods. Along with some of their family members, including Aleksander's daughter Asta and some close friends, they were also escaping in their own boat.

Ours was an open fishing boat about seven meters long (or about twenty-one feet) with about a three-to-five-horsepower motor. The top of the boat was still open, as there was no time to cover it with the canvas that had been brought along.

The night was darkening when we all squeezed like sardines into the deep bottom of our boat, facing each other, with our heads up and feet together. Looking back toward the coast and Haapsalu, we saw fires and smoke here and there. We knew that we had escaped "just in time" as we headed for the little island called Liia seven kilometers away. There were already several other boats as we docked there for the night. The women and children spent the night in bunk beds on hay mattresses in a summer cabin and the men in the hay barn, used by hay harvesters and fishermen during the summer.

Now it was September 24 and it was Sunday. No Sunday in our lives had ever been like this. We wondered if people back at home would be gathering in our church, confused, wondering where the pastor and family were. Or was anyone going to church that morning since maybe the communists' tanks and trucks were filling the roads?

The men of our boat had been working furiously since the wee hours of the morning to get the canvas cover securely fastened to the boat and everything ready for the long journey. Meanwhile, Mr. Rannus had been studying the heavy seas, the upcoming weather, and our small boat with its weak motor. He decided that he and his wife did not want to risk their lives and announced that they would return home! One of Tikas's relatives, a young mother named Leida Kink and her small daughter, Tiia, were trying to escape on another way-overcrowded boat, so they came into our boat.

But what a shock it was for us! Because none of our men had the navigational experience or skills needed, a replacement for Mr. Rannus, who was to be our helmsman, had to be found immediately. Papa walked around as we prayed that God somehow would lead someone to us. He spotted two young men, Peeter Kaups and his friend Heino, wandering around. Since he knew Peeter's father, Karl, who was the head of our Baptist denomination, he asked Peeter, who was originally from the Island of Hiiumaa, if he could handle our boat across the sea. His parents, who had been waiting for him and his friend to make the journey with them to Sweden, had finally given up and left in their yacht.

So here were Peeter and Heino looking to hitch a ride and Peeter reluctantly responded, "I will make an attempt, but only if you can also accommodate my friend Heino." Praise God, the Krabi brothers had just enough room to fit Heino into their boat, and again, God was faithful in providing a way, this time through twenty-one-year-old Peeter becoming our helmsman!

As it became evening, all of the boats departed along with ours, but unfortunately, somewhere in the darkness, we lost our course trying to avoid rocks and shallows, and Peeter turned the boat back to Liia Islet where we spent the night in the boat.

The Russian forces reached Haapsalu on that day but apparently did not have the ships or boats to pursue the refugees fleeing by sea.

Very early in the morning of September 25, the wind picked up as we set out west toward the island of Hanikats, over twenty kilometers away. As the storm gathered, we pulled in there where several other boats were already docked. No one attempted to continue but stayed to wait out the storm, which was becoming quite fierce.

There were two deaf-mute families living on the beautiful Hanikats Island. They were very kind to the refugees, allowing some of the women and children to sleep in their houses on hay sacks on the floor and others in the barns on straw. It was raining most of the time and the sea was stormy. We stayed there for nearly three days to wait out the storm. As our food was getting scarce, we picked mushrooms and wild berries in the woods.

It seemed that our "captain" Peeter and Asta Krabi from her family's boat were starting a little romance—we girls would watch them walking together now and then and thought they made a nice pair. (They married each other in Stockholm in February 1946 in a double wedding with our cousin Viktor and his former university friend Lydia Burmeister).

Our Escape

On September 28, a boat arrived with a couple of fishermen aboard. They brought news from the mainland that the Russians were already in Virtsu (a port town on the mainland) and had taken over most of the land. The fishermen told us they were headed for Saaremaa. When Leida from our boat heard this, she wanted to go with them, since her husband was there waiting for her and their little daughter, Tiia, so we parted ways.

Much later, we found out that these "fishermen," instead of going to Saaremaa, headed right back to the mainland. Meanwhile, Leida's husband could not wait any longer and had made his way to Sweden, so the family was separated for life. Fifty years later, on the night between September 27-28 1994, after Estonia had become free, Tiia was on the cruise ferry ship *Estonia* on her way to visit her father in Sweden for the first time since his escape in 1944. One of the worst maritime disasters of the century occurred in the frigid waters of the Baltic Sea, when that ferry sank with 460 cars and 852 passengers on board. Sadly, most of the people, including Tiia, perished in the fierce storm between Tallinn and Stockholm and the two were never able to see each other again. Tiia's mother by that time was dead.

On Friday, September 29, around midday when the storm had ceased, we continued our travel to Pihla Island, located between Hiiumaa and Saaremaa, but closer to Saaremaa, over thirty kilometers away. Several boats had gathered. Some of the people had made a campfire on the small island. We, too, went ashore to stretch our legs and eat.

The open sea was ahead of us to the west, and the sun was setting behind dark clouds when we prayed before getting back into the boat. There was no more time to wait. We knew we had to make our escape. Our boat started out with all the other boats from Pihla Isalnd, but soon they all disappeared into the darkness among the gathering waves. We started singing an old familiar hymn, "Jesus Savior pilot me, over life's tempestuous sea. Unknown waves before me roll, Hiding rocks and treach'rous shoals. Chart and compass come from Thee, Jesus Savior, pilot me!" ("*Armas Jeesus tüüri sa, Meie laeva hoolega. Vii meid läbi suurest veest, hoia õnnetuse eest. Kui Su käsi tüüri peab, Küll siis sadamasse saab.*") That night, this song took on a brand new meaning.

Our goal was the nearest Swedish shore, perhaps Sandhamn, about 250 kilometers (around 160 miles) nearly west on the other side of the turbulent Baltic Sea from our last stop at Pihla Island. At one point after we had been at sea for perhaps an hour, we saw a submarine submerge and wondered what would happen next. Apparently they didn't see us or did not bother to worry about us. Most likely it belonged to Germans.

We did not know that the most difficult portion of our escape had begun. If one estimates that the boat's speed in calm water was maybe 10-15 kilometers per hour (6-9 mph), then with the boat heavily loaded with passengers and stormy seas, the most optimistic prediction would have been that we would arrive the following night, after at least a twenty-four-hour trip. But the voyage turned out to be much more eventful and filled with hardship.

As we continued, the sea got rougher and rougher. The boat was rocking up and down with the waves. The larger waves came perhaps twenty or thirty seconds apart, and smaller ones came more frequently. The boat creaked and shuddered with each push of the waves but it held fast and kept the churning green mass of water from getting into the boat. As the wind increased, waves began to break and water sprayed over and splashed into the boat. Cousin Viktor and Aleksander Reins continually took turns pumping out the water with a hand pump as they sat by the opening in the back of the canvas that covered the boat, acting as a human barrier to keep as much of the water as possible from entering in.

Underneath the canvas, the rest of us were tense and continued to pray. At the same time, to keep ourselves calm, we sang many, many Estonian Christian songs that talk about the stormy sea with its rolling waves on the sea of life, like: ("*Me purjetame hirmsaa maru käes, Maailma mere peal . . . Oo Jeesus tüüri meie laeva Sa ja juhata meid sadamasse ka, Kus Rahumaa, Kus Rahumaa, Kus 'Rootsimaa'*") and many other songs.

It was getting to be more and more painful just to stay half-lying there on our backs or sitting on the bottom of the boat so tightly close to each other with just a blanket underneath. From time to time during the night, I dozed off, but just as quickly I woke up to hear the endless sound of the roaring sea.

On Saturday, September 30, the wind increased and the storm became even more fierce. The wind had been blowing steadily from the southwest over the entire length of the Baltic Sea. Waves had grown into extremely high mountains of water. The height from wave crest to trough, in Peeter's estimation, was about 10-12 meters (35-40 feet) or even more. At one point as I peeked out, it was like a high dark wall of a huge building! Then one of these massive waves broke onto the boat! Water spewed throughout the boat and gushed through our clothes!

"Help! Help!" Panic and confusion gripped us! I clung to Ester next to me! "Are we going to perish!? Oh, God, help us, help us! Save us!" we cried.

The men immediately started bailing out water with whatever container or scoop was around. Surely the end must be near. To lighten the load, most of our belongings were tossed overboard, including the big milk container of drinking water. Then the water-soaked motor stopped and with it, my heart seemed to stop, too.!

Now what? For a while we just drifted and were tossed where the waves took us. It was feared that the storm might push us into the Gulf of Finland and back into Russian hands.

Our motorist, Jaan, worked laboriously with the motor and finally got it working with partial power. The storm, however, grew stronger and any forward progress with a poorly working motor was hopeless. Now at the mercy of the storm, the boat just drifted with the wind in a direction that seemed completely away from the planned course—not that that mattered much anymore . . .

Suddenly, during the second night, our three guys at the open back end of the boat all started shouted, "There's a light flickering way up ahead, quick! We have to get their attention!"

Some pieces of cloth were dipped and soaked in gasoline and lit like a torch, and the men waved them, but no response to this signal came. It is difficult to guess what light this may have been, as the men could see the light only for the brief moments when the boat was on top of the wave crests. In all likelihood, this was a ship, maybe even a warship, or perhaps a lighthouse on a distant shore or island, but at that point, no one could guess where we were or how far we had traveled.

We felt miserable, hopeless, and despairing, yet our fearless, brave boatman kept his hand steady at the helm. We kept praying for him, and as death seemed so near, we knew our only real hope was Jesus.

On Sunday, October 1, our journey continued on the stormy sea. We still faced mountainous waves and cloudy skies . . . *Where will we land? Will we land anywhere at all?* No food or water remained and we experienced a peculiar constant nausea, an aching body, and wet clothes.

Finally in the late afternoon, flat, rocky islands came into sight! Some even had a few scraggly trees on them. Peeter steered the boat in among the islands. The waves quieted and the boat was moored next to an island with some small juniper trees in hopes that we would find inhabitants here. It was already dark. But where were we? No identifying landmark could be seen.

Viktor and Onu Reins got out and went ashore, but when Peeter stood up after steering for forty-eight hours straight, he was so stiff that he fell overboard. The men pulled him out and everyone got back in the boat. Yes, we spent another painful night with cold, wet clothes in the crowded and, by now, smelly boat. Yet sighs of relief and thankfulness rose to our heavenly Father that we were in the shelter of an island and had escaped thus far with our lives.

On the morning of Monday, October 2, we all went ashore, hoping to find some signs of life . . . but the only "tracks" we found were what the sheep had left behind after apparently grazing here during summer. We made a small fire and collected water from hollows in the rocks (with the sheep remains pushed aside). We made a kind of tea from juniper berries that we gathered and sugar, which was wet from being in a paper bag, but at least the tea was warm. Onu Tikas jokingly made a comment about the sugar, saying, "If we haven't learned anything else on this journey, it's the fact that one should never bring sugar in a paper bag when going out to sea!"

In the afternoon we saw a fishing boat passing the island in the distance. After we were able to get their attention by waving a white shirt, they pulled ashore. They were Finnish-Swedes and Peeter, who spoke Finnish, was able to tell them about our predicament. They explained that we had landed on the Finnish Ahvenamaa Islands (Aland Islands), about 180-200 kilometers (115-125 miles) northwest of Pihla Island. Of course, we had really traveled a much longer distance as we were pushed and stranded "all over" the Baltic Sea.

The fishermen were friendly, and they took our boat in tow. After a couple of hours, we reached their home on another island. Here they had a comfortable living and invited us all in. Soon their women had tables set and fed us fish, potatoes with gravy, bread, milk, and fruit soup for dessert. We were so hungry and everything tasted *so* good.

Thankfulness to God filled our hearts for bringing us here to safety and leading us to these dear people. Our group was divided up to sleep in the different homes of the fishermen. Our whole family was able to sleep in one home . . . oh, what a comfortable night, to be in a warm bed with sheets and blankets after such hardships during the previous days and nights.

My Father's Guiding Hand

On the morning of Tuesday, October 4, the whole group was invited back to the house where we were guests—for coffee, oatmeal, rye bread, and fish. They gave us a large bag of hard-tack rye bread (*knäckebröd*) for the journey ahead. (For me, *knäckebröd* symbolizes life and sustenance and I will forever be grateful when I pick up this kind of bread.) The fishermen helped to get the boat motor back into working order. Midmorning, we bid farewell to our hosts and resumed our travel, navigating between the hundreds of small rocky islands for five or six hours toward a border control point with the fishermen leading the way. They had already radioed the lighthouse crew ahead that a refugee boat was en route.

When we arrived at our destination, the Finnish border guards greeted us warmly as we docked our boat and then climbed up one side of the high rocky island's steep steps to their living quarters. Here was a good-sized mess hall, kitchen, and bedrooms for the men. They joyously handed over the kitchen to our women, who fixed fish soup for all of us for dinner that night. We slept on the floor of the mess hall. On the advice of the seasoned seamen, we stayed another day to wait for the present storm to blow over. For meals, along with our ladies, they prepared pan-fried smelt, potatoes, and tea. On our second evening, we sang and Papa led the evening devotions and prayer, with the border guards joining us.

Our Escape

On Thursday, October 5, very early in the morning, the chief border guard had been notified that orders had come for the detention of refugees because the Finnish-Soviet Armistice Treaty required the Finns to keep any Estonian refugees and hand them over to the Soviets. We had to leave almost immediately. Although the wind had moderated, a stiff breeze was still blowing and the seas were rough for our small boat. The border guards took our boat in tow behind their own fast motorboat, quickly towing us to the edge of Finnish territorial waters.

From there, we continued on under our own power. After several hours, we saw a Swedish warship that soon approached us and their crew took our boat in tow. Apparently, they contacted a smaller Swedish border-guard vessel, since after a while we saw this approaching. Their plan was to transfer us to the smaller ship, but in the course of maneuvers, our little boat was somewhat crushed between the two ships (but not destroyed)! We were quickly pulled up to the war ship and later moved to the smaller one. What a relief to be onboard a Swedish vessel. We were given hot chocolate, sweets, and oranges and at last felt safe!

We traveled for a couple more hours toward Sweden on the border-guard ship and by evening we were taken to a refugee camp on Furusund Island. There all thirteen of us had to register before being escorted to the dining hall of a nice summer hotel where many Estonian refugees had already been brought. Everything was so light! No more black-outs! Long tables with white (paper) tablecloths were set up with plenty of food. I will never forget this sight! Tears welled up in my eyes. It felt like we had arrived in heaven and I could almost imagine Jesus coming and saying, "Come and dine!"

There was a freedom in my heart that I can't describe! No more fear of communism. Twelve days had passed since we had left home. God's hand had truly and miraculously protected and guided us through dreadful autumn storms in our little vessel. Now we were actually in a free land! Thank You, Lord!

Chapter 8

Sweden – Refugee Camps ∽

For most of the summer, the resort area on Furusund Island had been used as a refugee camp and gathering place. Our group was assigned to Hotel Dagmar, which had no heating system, and since the weather was getting cooler, some days later the women and children were placed in another hotel called Liidu. However, Papa, along with other men, was placed in different smaller summer cottages.

At first, the weather was still warm and sunny, and the changing fall colors were beautiful. We girls walked to the waterfront to visit Papa and to explore the island and the woods where we found a tiny cottage that was like a big barrel turned on its side. What a perfect place to play! There were "bench-beds" on either side and a small table by the tiny window. The children to whom it must belong probably came here to play every summer since it was nice and clean with even a lace curtain on the window.

There were several Swedish "*lotas*" (nurses' aides) who came to "our" hotel every morning to dispense spoonfuls of cod-liver oil to each of the children. That taste and smell were so horrible that whenever we possibly could, we would run outside behind a corner and spit it out!

Being the singers that we are, we gathered other kids and sang Estonian patriotic songs. Then we discovered that there was a music teacher among us, who began teaching and directing our choir. Every now and then we would entertain the rest of the people in the dining hall. But when nighttime came, we especially missed being together with Papa, our home in Estonia, and all that was dear to our hearts.

Over the next days and weeks, ships left steadily from Furusund to take refugees to other parts of Sweden. Most of our group was separated and left at different times. Our family stayed in Furusund until October 28.

On that morning we too got on a ship that took us to Stockholm. We had already heard about what was to come. It was nicknamed "lice hell" (*täipõrgu*). Here we were brought into a giant bathhouse. The men were separated from women and children and were led to different "cleaning areas." After being told to undress, we were lined up to get this yucky stuff put in our hair by a Swedish "*lota*" or nurses' aide. Then we were sent into a hot sauna to sit there for quite a while. After that came a disinfecting soaping and back into the sauna. After another shower, everyone was thoroughly disinfected from any lice or fleas that one may have brought into this clean land. Finally, we received a bag with fresh, clean used clothes from head to toe— and that did feel wonderful.

"I am a refugee" in Sweden 1945

From Stockholm we were transported through the well-lit city by bus to a long train that took us to a refugee camp in Kvicksund, near Eskilstuna (located south of Stockholm) and right by Lake Mälare, the third largest lake in Sweden.

Here was a large two story hotel-like house with a big dining room and other hotel rooms that were divided between the refugees. Our family, together with Papa, however, was placed in a small cottage right next to the hotel. On one end of this cottage was our room, and in one of the other rooms across our entryway, was a bigger room where several bachelors, including our cousin Viktor, stayed. Even though we were quite crowded in our room, it was so nice to be together again as a whole family.

Soon we found out that among the refugees were quite a few children and also a schoolteacher. He organized a few classes for us during the week. Since the age difference was so varied among the children, it was a bit hard, but we even got to learn a few words in Swedish. Of course we did some singing again, and with Christmas approaching, we started practicing Estonian Christmas songs and learned "*Nu är det jul igen*" ("Now It's Christmas Again") in Swedish. Later we learned that our Swedish pronunciation was really bad and that this song was to be sung at a much faster rhythm and speed! But when we performed at our Christmas program, the rest of the Estonians didn't know the difference, and the Swedish camp staff only smiled nicely as everyone clapped. The children were all given chocolates and little gifts.

On another day close to Christmas, we were taken by bus to a Swedish school Christmas party where we performed Estonian songs as a group. Ester and Hulda also sang a duet, and I sang a solo on all the verses, with all the Estonian children joining in at the chorus. Then the Swedish children sang for us as well, but we didn't think their singing was as good as ours because they all sang just the melody and didn't harmonize or sing parts, and some of the boys were off-key. After that, they all gathered around the Christmas tree holding hands and they started singing and "dancing" around the tree. Some of the songs also had different motions. We were invited to join in, but of course we didn't know any of their songs; still it was fun doing this together. Afterwards they treated us to cookies and punch.

Back "home" in our room, we did have a little Christmas tree. We made colorful paper chains and little baskets woven out of shiny colored paper the way we had learned to make them in Estonia. On Christmas Eve, we were all happy together. Papa and Mamma had gifts for us wrapped under the tree—colored pencils, writing pads, a chocolate for us to share, hankies for each of the girls, and a picture book for Kaljo. During our prayer time, however, we were all crying and missing our "real home in Ridala" and wondering if our relatives were even able to celebrate Christmas under communism . . . there was no way we could find out.

After Christmas, the weather got really cold. We refugees had to abide by the rules as to where we could go—we were limited to about half a kilometer around the camp. We were able to walk across the street to a kiosk with an automatic candy and goodie machine where one could put money in to get your choice of candy. The Swedish government gave each adult one kroon per week as "spending money," but as we needed to buy toothpaste, shampoo, and such, understandably there was no money for candy.

We were also allowed to cross the bridge by road that took us to the other side of a narrow part of Lake Mälare. Right there across the bridge was a store where a large beautiful model ship was on display. Kaljo had eyed this ship with longing eyes, but we had no means to buy this for him. Some days later, Kaljo noticed that our cousin Viktor, across the hall, had left his coat jacket on the back of a chair in our room and Kaljo had seen him put some money into his right-hand coat pocket.

As soon as everyone had left the room for the dining hall, Kaljo quickly reached his hand in that pocket and took out a 1 kroon Swedish coin. After lunch, with the coin in hand, he ran out and marched across the bridge, repeating "*shepet, shepet, shepet*" to himself (he had asked someone earlier how to say ship in Swedish) and hoped to reach his dream. Well, when he entered the store he said "shepet" while pointing at the ship and handing the store clerk his 1 kroon coin. The man shook his head and explained in Swedish that the "shepet" cost a lot more than 1 kroon! With tears in his eyes, our five-year-old Kaljo ran back.

That evening during our prayertime, he was very edgy and then, bursting into tears, he confessed his sins of stealing, sneaking out, and going without permission to the store to get the "*shepet*" and then not even getting it. He has never forgotten that incident (and the lessons of coveting, stealing, and going behind his parents' backs).

Quite often Mamma was on kitchen duty as the women helped with preparation and clean-up. Every morning we got runny oatmeal with milk and *knäcke-*

bröd with cheese; for lunch we usually had sandwiches or soup, and for dinner there was either fish, meatloaf, or soup. I remember that every Thursday we had pea soup with oven-baked pancakes for dessert. There was actually no lack of food, and children sometimes also got an apple.

After some Swedish Christians made contact with us in the refugee camp, Papa was given permission to visit them in Eskesltuna, the nearest large town. When he came back, he told us that a Swedish family would like to have Hulda come and live with them so she could learn Swedish. They had a couch in their hallway that opened up where Hulda could sleep at night and be like a big sister to their nine-year old daughter, Dagmar. During the week while Dagmar was at school and her parents were working, Hulda got to earn a little pocket money with another family by taking care of a two-year-old boy named Kjell while his parents were at work.

Soon after that, we learned that a missionary family near Eskelstuna wanted Ester to come and clean their house and do other chores around their home, so she also left us. Ester was fourteen at the time and Hulda was fifteen, and it was hard for them to be separated from our family for any length of time. They looked forward to seeing each other on Sundays since the two families attended the same Baptist church in Eskelstuna. Hulda's new family, the Eriksons, were very nice to her. On the other hand, Ester's missionary family, Thomassons, had two teenage boys who often teased her, laughing when she couldn't pronounce Swedish words right, or playing pranks on her.

From the refugee camp in Kvicksund, little by little, people were being placed to work on farms, in lumber camps, factories, etc., to start life on their own. In February, the Kvicksund camp was closed, and when Papa, Mama, Kaljo, and I were to be sent to another camp, Ester left the missionary family and joined us. It was located further south inland and was called Ribingelund.

This was a camp altogether different from our previous ones. Here were many long barracks. Inside, bunk beds lined the walls from one end to the other. Men were placed into "men's only" barracks and women and children were located at the other side of the camp. The bunk beds had paper mattresses filled with wood chips and paper "blankets." Between each set of bunks was a narrow closet for all of our belongings. People tried to get some kind of privacy, especially when dressing and undressing, by hanging a paper sheet at the end and sides of the beds. The food was awful as well as scarce.

It often snowed and the barracks got very cold. The only activity for us was to walk around the pathways between the barracks. Because the women and children were not allowed into the men's barracks and usually the meals were also served at different times, we seldom got to see Papa. The women were assigned different days for kitchen duty, and sometimes Mamma managed to bring us a little extra food. Every now and then we got a letter from Hulda, telling us about her life with the Swedish family and how she was able to go to church with them and had made a few friends. However, she missed being with us and we not only missed her very much, but also we missed Estonia, our home, and church more and more.

Fortunately, we didn't have to stay in Ribingelund for too long. Toward spring, the five of us were sent by train to yet another camp in the southern state of Småland to a little hamlet called Östergorsberga. Here another Estonian refugee camp had been set up in an insane asylum called Vänham. Most of the Swedish patients had been moved elsewhere, but some still remained in the third floor attic rooms where none of us were allowed to go.

At times, when Kaljo, I, and some other children in the camp were playing in the backyard, we saw these people longingly looking out of their windows. Several times, we saw one lady who came to the window with a little bundle in her arms. We could tell that this was not a real baby or even a doll, but that she had bundled up some clothing to resemble a baby. She cuddled it and kissed it . . . perhaps at some point in her life she had lost a baby and was still grieving. We wished we could go and just be nice to her and maybe relieve her loneliness.

My Father's Guiding Hand

In this large building, the doors of all the rooms on the second floor were about 10 cm thick and the windows had metal bars on them. Most of these rooms were already filled with Estonian refugees and with the arrival of our group, the place was filled to capacity. We, however, were placed on the ground floor with regular doors and windows, but the room itself was very small for our family of five. Mamma again took turns with kitchen duty as she had in other camps.

Ester and I had both missed a year of school but now, toward the end of April, we began attending Swedish grade school in this little hamlet about 1.5 kilometers away from Vänham. Since Kaljo was not quite six, he hung around with Papa during the day. We had been able to learn only a few words of Swedish in the refugee camps, and mostly we just sat and listened in school.

By now, I was eleven years old and was placed in the third grade. Ester went to the sixth grade at age fifteen, as this was the highest grade in the local school. Mainly this allowed us to get exposure to the language. Oh, how hard this was! Everything was so confusing. The man teacher for our third grade was quite kind, but the most vocal Swedish boys teased us saying, "You dumb Estonian refugees, go home!" We soon learned to understand what these words meant.

In class, I was actually able to participate in math, as numbers are numbers in any language, as long as it didn't involve written math problems. The fun times in school were the art and music classes. In art class I was given my own pastel colors of a kind I had never had before, and in music class I learned many Swedish songs; those just seemed to come naturally to me. One of the first songs that I learned was called "*Flickorna i Småland*" ("Girls in Småland") since we were residing in the Province of Småland, and another song was "*I Sommarens Soliga Dagar*" ("On Summer's Sunny Days"). The chorus of that song is sung so fast that it became quite a challenge to master!

Each day school began with morning prayer, as well as a class in religion, where such things as the Lord's Prayer, the benediction, the Confession of Faith for the Lutheran church, and some Bible stories were taught. This was a "*kyrko skola*" or church school. It was the public school for all the children in the area and next door was a big white stone Lutheran church.

During recess and lunch hour, the kids played soccer or some other ball games outside, but most of the time the boys didn't allow the younger kids to play. In Ester's grade, there were two Estonian boys who were very good with the ball and would sometimes get it and pass it along to other Estonian kids. But mostly I sat on the sidelines with the not-so-popular girls and watched other girls play marbles or hopscotch.

As the snow melted, Papa, with his gardening background in Estonia, was put to work on the grounds, planting flowers and taking care of the large yard surrounding the buildings. By now, many Estonians in the camp had been leaving as they found work in different parts of Sweden wherever the Swedish language was not required and rented rooms wherever they could. With so many refugees in the country, there was quite a housing shortage although most refugees couldn't afford much anyway. Many shared rooms with different families, but at least it was a new beginning.

Mamma was also able to get a job in a sewing factory fourteen kilometers away in the nearest town called Vetlanda. She rented a room on the upper floor from a Swedish family and she stayed there during the week and was able to take the train to join us Saturday evenings after work, staying until Sunday evenings.

At the beginning of the summer, this Estonian refugee camp as such ended. World War II also ended in May of 1945.

Chapter 9

More Moves

We found a little summer cottage to rent a couple of kilometers from Vänhem where Papa was still working as the gardener, now for minimum pay, while Mamma continued to work in Vetlanda. To our great joy, Hulda came by train from Eskelstuna where she had lived with the Swedish family. She now spoke fluent Swedish. It was so good to have her with us. We had not seen her since Christmas.

This little "*röda stugan*" or red cottage was about a quarter kilometer from the road in the woods. We had just the minimum of used furniture, but it was so special to be here since Saturday evenings and on Sundays we were all together again as a family. Our dear friends, Maria and Jüri Tikas, who had escaped with us from Estonia, also came to spend the summer. Tädi Tikas cooked and we all helped around the cottage while

125

Mamma and Papa were at work. With school being out, Kaljo was glad to have his sisters play and run around outside with him. Every day we went to the woods to pick berries to help with the food budget. Often other Estonians came to visit us on weekends, and we had our "church services." There were no Swedish evangelical churches in the area.

As summer ended, life changed again. Because the little summer cottage was not winterized, it was too cold for us to stay in. Ester and Hulda joined Mamma in her little upstairs rented room in Vetlanda where they started attending the local high school.

Ester, Hulda, Mairy –
Summer 1945

Papa with Kaljo and Mairy
living in Vänham, Sweden

Papa, Kaljo, and I moved back to Vänhem, except now to a house next to where the Estonian camp had been. Here we had a slightly larger room on the second floor. Downstairs and on the other end of the upstairs lived nonviolent Swedish mental patients. Papa continued working as the gardener/caretaker. I returned to the same Swedish grade school, again in third grade, as I hadn't passed the grade with my very limited Swedish the previous spring when I had attended for less than two months of the school year. For our meals, we walked over to the big building as we had no kitchen facilities of our own except an electric hot plate to heat water or for minimum cooking.

At Vänhem, however, a new camp was set up where Jews who had survived the Nazi concentration camps in Germany, Austria, and elsewhere in Europe were brought. These were mostly Hungarians, Czechoslovakians, or Bulgarian Jews. We learned about their plight and heard their horrid stories. Each one had a tattooed number on his or her upper left arm. They had lost most of their families but were glad to be alive.

Papa had always told us, "If you bless God's chosen people, the Jews, God will bless you." So here we were being "blessed" by Jews and getting to celebrate their holidays, such as Hanukkah, Purim, and Passover, and often eating kosher food at the same table. Most of them spoke German, and Papa enjoyed conversing with them. During the Jewish Passover, since there was no Jewish rabbi among them, they gave Papa a skullcap and asked him to lead in their Seder, telling the Old Testament meaning of the Passover. Each time I passed the living room that housed a piano, one of these guys would be pounding out a Jewish tune like "Ha Tikvah" that talked about the hope and longing for a free homeland, Israel (which later became their national anthem). I learned to sing "Hava Nagila" from them, a popular and catchy Jewish song in Hebrew and also learned to speak some Hebrew words as well as to count to ten in Hungarian. Living among different nationalities really enriched our lives.

December came and on the thirteenth we had a St. Lucia Day celebration at school. For St. Lucia Day, the most beautiful blonde, long-haired girl from school was chosen to be St. Lucia. She wore a long white dress with a red sash, depicting the martyr's death of St. Lucia. On her head she wore a crown of white live candles as she walked into the auditorium with her court of several other girls all dressed in long white gowns, carrying white candles and singing the St. Lucia song. ("*Natten går tynga fjäll, rund gård och stuva*"). After them came the "*tomtegubbar*" or little elves with bright red hats and costumes who helped pass around cookies and St. Lucia sweetbreads. The teachers also got coffee. This is a Swedish tradition and brings in the Christmas season at this dark time of the year with the light of Jesus Christ to lighten the world. In towns and cities, it is celebrated with parades and people making a chain by holding on to each other's hands, running along the streets, and then ending up in the town square to dance around the huge Christmas tree. Hulda and Ester really enjoyed all of this with their Swedish high school friends in Vetlanta where they got to join in all the Lucia Day celebrations.

When Christmas arrived, Hulda, Ester, and Mamma, as on most weekends, came to our one-room "home" where our family celebrated Christmas 1945. That winter and into spring it was hard to continue to live apart as a family and still not have Mamma with us during the week. I struggled with my studies with a Swedish-Estonian dictionary in one hand and a textbook in the other, trying to figure it all out one word at a time in order to do my homework each evening. But little by little, I began to understand Swedish more and more. Kaljo was still too young to be in school, there were no other children with whom to play so it was hard for him as well to just hang around and help Papa while he worked.

We had applied for an apartment that was being built in Vetlanda so we could move there as a family. The notice finally came from the owner in late spring that the apartment we would rent was finished and we could move in! I well remember that the address was Vasagatan 46, Vetlanda.

On our moving day, the sun was shining and the two-room apartment with large windows looked so big and bright. Hulda and Ester were to sleep on the pullout couch in the living room and Papa, Mamma, Kaljo, and I in the bedroom. The kitchen had electric appliances and was big enough for a table and six chairs. We had our own bathroom with a sink, toilet, and bathtub. In the basement was a sauna and a laundry room with bigger sinks where we could wash our clothes by hand. We were so grateful to God to finally have a "home" where we could all be together as a family and have this much room.

I finished third grade in a new school, and in spite of all the new circumstances, I adjusted quite well. Papa got a job at a garden center owned by a Christian family, and Mamma continued her work at the sewing factory. We attended a Swedish Baptist church on Sundays and learned Swedish hymns, many of which have the same melodies as our Estonian hymns.

Summer came and Ester, too, got work at the garden center and Hulda at a factory. Kaljo and I made friends with local Swedish kids. In the fall as school began again, I started the fourth grade and was doing much better. At age seven, the required age in Sweden, Kaljo began school in the first grade and Ester and Hulda continued in high school.

In October Papa received a letter from some Estonian friends living in Nyköping, a town north of us and closer to Stockholm, asking him to come and preach there to a group of Estonian Christians for a weekend. A few weeks later, after Papa had made the journey by train, he came back with the news that this group of believers wanted him to come and be their pastor. The understanding was that there was to be no specific salary, only whatever anyone could put in the collection plate, as they were all refugees beginning new lives. Of course we prayed about this, but Papa hardly hesitated to accept the call, as he knew this was God's work and He would provide.

So that fall, in November, we made yet another move, leaving our nice apartment in Vetlanda to move further north to Nyköping. Actually, the place where Papa, Mamma, and Hulda got work was three kilometers outside the city of Nyköping in a hamlet called Harg. Papa got a job as a maintenance man at a large textile factory, working from five in the morning until two in the afternoon, with Mamma and Hulda working the afternoon/evening shift from 2:00 to 10:00 p.m. on large textile machines. Each week the morning and evening shifts were reversed. The factory provided housing for rent in the village in tiny separate wooden barracks for each household.

We arrived in Nyköping by train with our few belongings on a dark and dreary evening, hardly able to believe that this is where we would be living. As we entered the small barrack's hallway, on the right was what was to be Kaljo's and my "room" with about a two-foot-wide passageway to walk in. At the end of the passageway was a closet of the same width and a narrow bunk bed by the wall. On the left side of the hall was the narrow kitchen with a stove, sink, and a couple of cupboards with no room for a table or anything else. From the hallway, straight ahead was the "living room" area with a pullout couch for Hulda and Ester, a table and four chairs, and by one wall was a stove to heat the place with wood. Behind this wall was Papa and Mamma's "room" with the same setup as Kaljo's and mine, except the two narrow beds were on the floor next to each other with the small passageway on each side and the narrow closets on each end. The walls throughout this small barrack were made of wood, and the only door was the front door to the house and one for the kitchen. For bathroom facilities we had to go outside past several other barracks to a "community washroom" that had several stalls with two sinks and two showers. On the other side of this washroom barrack, the facilities for men were about the same. (Oh, oh, oh . . . never will I forget when I was sick to my stomach and had to make my way out there in the snow several times during the night!)

As we looked around our new "home," a sadness filled the place. Then Hulda spoke up with a cheerful voice, "Oh, look, this is like a little dollhouse! Look, we can put the Christmas tree right here and move the couch this way, and we can probably find a box from somewhere to make a bookcase here!" (Yes, definitely imagination.) Mamma said, "Let me find the pot and put some hot tea on . . ."

Our new life here had begun. Ester started high school in Nyköping, and Kaljo and I went to school in Harg, about 1.5 kilometers away. This was a small country school and my teacher, *Fröken* (Miss) Dolly, was a very special lady who made each of the children feel that they, too, were special. She was most interested in how I had gotten to Sweden and was eager to make me feel a part of the class. Because by now I spoke Swedish fluently, and before spring without any accent, people couldn't even tell that I wasn't a Swede. My favorite subject beside music and art was history, and I wanted to find out all about Swedish history, a fourth-grade subject. At home, since we were all so crowded, I did my homework on my top bunk and since I was quite short, at the foot of my bed I had a small wooden box that served as my bookcase. This was the place for all my books, artwork, and personal things.

Every Sunday we went to the Estonian church in Nyköping that Papa now pastored. The people met in a Swedish Baptist church building. Mamma started Sunday school with nearly twenty children. With Christmas approaching, we practiced songs and learned poems for the program and Papa started a choir.

In our little home, we did get a small Christmas tree as Hulda had dreamed. Even though we had hardly anything and were so cramped, our parents never let us feel that we were poor. Their attitude was always such that we were so very rich because we had Jesus and we were children of the King! As we once again celebrated the birth of Christ at church and at home, our gifts, as usual, were very modest, and yet the joy of sharing and the little surprises were somehow all special. Mamma made Estonian-type Christmas food that we all enjoyed.

That New Year's Eve we had a clear night with a full moon and millions of stars brightly shining in the sky. We three girls went sledding with a group of Estonian kids in the neighborhood using our "kick sled" (as described in Estonia) that we had acquired while living in Vetlanda. Since almost everyone in Sweden also had these sleds, we could hook one sled to another, making a long "train" of several sleds. There was a good-sized hill near the barracks where we had a wonderful time that night with our friends, making many great runs. And as the saying goes, "When on New Year's Eve you ride much, you'll be going far that year . . ." So ended the year 1946, and 1947 arrived!

Our four siblings on a kick-sled

In the first part of the new year, we were awestruck when an unusual postcard arrived for us in the mail! We could have no communication with our relatives or anyone back in Estonia where Russia ruled with an iron fist. Sometime after we had gotten to Sweden, Papa had sent a brief postcard to our grandmother with no return address, thinking that she would be the most neutral person to let our relatives know that we were alive and had made it here by posting it with a Swedish stamp. We knew their lives would be in danger if they corresponded with a foreign country. We had no idea whether that postcard ever reached her or if the communists had destroyed it.

Finally now, nearly two and half years later, Vanaema wrote back, addressing her postcard in Ester's name; it had been written on October 25, 1946. We did not know where her postcard had been for the nearly three months it took to reach Sweden, how long the communist officials had held and censored it, nor where she got the address of the Baptist Tabernacle in Stockholm. In Stockholm, however, her letter was given to an Estonian pastor, Dr. Artur Proos, who in turn had handed it to our cousin Viktor (who also lived in Stockholm) and he then sent it on to us in Harg.

Vanaema wrote that this was her third postcard to us, that her eyes were nearly dry from crying so much, and she was concerned about whether we had enough bread to eat! She asked Ester to greet everyone and signed it

"Vanaema." (Who knows how long it had taken for our postcard to reach her?) Surely she and the family had been praying and crying, not knowing if we had perished at sea. Still, at some point she must have received Papa's postcard in order to know to write to us in Sweden.

Perhaps the only reason her third card finally reached us was that Vanaema knew that this was "good propaganda" to write about her concern for the lack of bread and was hopeful that perhaps this was a way for the communists to allow her card to be sent. Our relatives all knew that if we had reached Sweden, there would be plenty of bread to eat here. At least now we knew that they were still living, but nothing more. We prayed for our loved ones more fervently than ever before . . . (Ester has kept Vanaema's postcard all these years).

In the winter, all of the Swedish kids went to school on skis, but of course we had none. One Sunday evening our family was invited for coffee to the home of a Swedish Christian family that owned a bakery in Harg. When we were already outside leaving for home, I noticed a pair of skis and poles sticking out of their garbage can beside the outside stairs. I asked Mamma, "Do you suppose we could ask if their daughter is throwing these away, maybe I could have them?"

So back inside we went, asked if this was possible, and sure enough, these became my skis. It didn't matter that the back end of one ski was slit partway in two, because when I stood on them, I could cover up the back end so no one would notice the broken ski. The next day I was off to school on my "new" skis. I don't even recall how, but soon Kaljo also got some skis from someone, so now we could both ski to school together.

During physical ed classes, there were ski races and, even though my skis weren't as good as the others', it was still fun to join in these activities and feel that I too "belonged."

Slowly spring arrived, and with the snow melting, all of the wildflowers in the woods came out. Like in Estonia, Sweden's woods are filled with beautiful wildflowers, which we loved to pick, bringing them home to brighten up our little barrack. We children had adjusted well, having made many friends among both the Swedes and Estonians.

Our Family in Sweden 1947

Sometime after we had arrived in Sweden in 1944, Papa had written to his two brothers and one sister who lived in the United States. During the war years in Estonia, he had not been able to be in contact with them. Our uncle Charlie and Uncle Walter (Volli) had left home by ship when they were in their teens to work with a relative in Cardiff, Wales. After some years, they had both immigrated to Canada, homesteaded in Alberta, and later worked in Vancouver, British Columbia in construction. By 1908, after earning enough money, Uncle Walter bought a sixty-three-acre piece of land in a little community called Hockinson in the foothills of the Cascade Mountain Range in the state of Washington. Uncle Charlie came to live in Portland, Oregon. Our Aunt Roosi and family (the ones who sent us packages now and then when we lived in Estonia) had settled in the Eastern part of the USA, mostly in the New York area.

As Papa, now in Sweden, began corresponding with his brothers and sister, they urged us to come to the United States. The quota for Estonians permitted to immigrate to the United States was so small that we would have had to wait more than twenty years. Even though being blood relatives we were able to forgo the regular quota, it still took nearly two years to complete all the paperwork, guarantees, visas, documents, and to purchase tickets and make that move. Finally everything was in order and the departure date for us to leave Sweden from Göteborg (Gothenburg) harbor was to be May 9, 1947.

We still wished we could go back to Estonia, but day by day this seemed more and more impossible. One could not travel back and forth, and even Sweden wasn't a safe place as, on the demand of Russia, hundreds of Estonian soldiers who had fought against the Russians in Estonian battalions in the German army but had somehow escaped to Sweden, had been sent back. This was such a painful procedure for the soldiers that as they were being dragged away to a Russian ship, some committed suicide. As a result, many Estonians were looking for ways to leave Sweden.

Leaving our barracks home in Sweden

Chapter 10

Our Big Move ❧

So once again, we were to pack our suitcases and this time end our life in Sweden. School was not yet out for summer break, nevertheless Fröken Dolly gave me a good report card and a beautiful amber-colored crystal bird as a going away gift that I still have to this day. My classmates gathered around me to say good-bye and my best friends there, Marianne, Barbro, and Ingrid, wanted to correspond with me.

In our Estonian barrack-village it was also hard to leave, since several of the kids had become my good friends. Ilme, Leida, and I used to play together in the village and we enjoyed going to a huge haystack nearby. Some of the boys, like Uno, Kaljo V., Mati, and Lembit, had made "tunnels" all the way to the top of the haystack and there we would read or just sit and talk.

On the night before we were to leave, I lost my watch in the haystack and didn't discover this until it was too dark to see anything. I could hardly sleep all night, worrying and praying. Very early the next morning, I went out there looking for it and, lo and behold, right by the haystack lay my watch! (It had been exactly like the saying goes: "looking for a needle in a haystack"!) Thank You, God!

On our last Sunday, our Estonian congregation, together with the Swedish Christians, gave our family a beautiful farewell in their church. They also gave us a leather album with handmade Estonian designs with everyone's pictures in it. The next morning, we left our barrack-home by taxi and boarded the train for Stockholm at the Nyköping railroad station. There were sad good-byes and a send-off with flowers. We stayed near Stockholm for a couple of days with our

I'm heading for America! Aboard the Drottningholm

142

cousin Viktor, who by now was married and living in a nice apartment by the water with his wife, Lydia. Then we took another train to Göteborg where we boarded the big Swedish ocean-liner *Drottningholm* on May 9.

It took us ten days to cross the Atlantic Ocean from Sweden to New York Harbor. Every day we went out on the deck from our cabins on the lowest deck and walked around. At first there were coastlines and islands to be seen, but then for days and days, there was nothing but sea and more sea. Inside, though, was a playroom where Kaljo spent quite a bit of time playing with the different toys and it was fun for me to also work there on some puzzles and to read. It was interesting as well to explore the big ship and to enjoy the excellent food in the dining room. However, one morning they had great big oranges, a little different color yellow from the orange ones that we had eaten before, but we dug right into the half that was cut on our plates. My, oh my, these were so sour we wondered what they were! Well, they turned out to be grapefruits instead—something we had never tasted before.

We did experience a storm while at sea and the old ship creaked and rolled with the huge waves. I got quite woozy with seasickness and missed some of the meals, and then I just stayed in our cabin. Papa and Ester endured the weather best of our family.

On the tenth day, May 19, everyone was up early. We all went out to the deck as someone called out, "We're coming to America!" Sure enough, we saw land ahead, and little by little, we got closer and closer to actually seeing the Statue of Liberty, which we recognized from pictures we had seen earlier. A kind of panic and wonder filled my heart—were we really coming to America?! This "wonderland" that we had heard so much about . . . My heart was beating fast as the ship docked in the harbor. We all ran downstairs to get our things and then back up again with our suitcases, as everybody was pushing their way ahead to get off.

We didn't have to go to the famous Ellis Island, where immigrants went through the long lines for screening and security, since our relatives were sponsoring us. Slowly we followed everyone up a long flight of stairs and waited for our turn. Some of the people ahead of us were pulled aside, as they apparently didn't have all their necessary documents. Fortunately for us, it went relatively fast since all the required papers were in order, and we had relatives waiting for us on the other side! Everything seemed like a dream.

Soon we greeted our cousin John Kusik, whom we children had never seen before and who had come to pick us up in a car. We learned that he was a graduate of Columbia University and now the vice president of the Chesapeake and Ohio Railroad Company in Cleveland, Ohio. He lived there with his wife, Gloria, from whom I got my middle name. Gloria had been a model for *Vogue* magazine when they met and were married. Now they had two children about my age.

John's sister, cousin Ella, with her husband, Max Brubaker, lived in a high-rise apartment in New York City and also came to meet us. They took Hulda and Ester with them. Then cousin John drove Papa, Mamma, Kaljo, and me to our cousin Erica and her husband Frank Dana's house on Long Island, where our aunt Roosi and uncle August lived with them. They had a nice fenced-in backyard where Kaljo and I got to play badminton and just relax after the eventful day. For the adults there was so much catching up to do after not seeing each other for so many years.

While in New York, we also saw another cousin, Helen (uncle Alexander's daughter), and her husband, Bill Kerson. Helen and Bill had no children and, because somehow she took a liking to me and hugged and kissed me a lot, I started calling her "*musi tädi*" ("kissing aunt"). Helen took us to the city where we met up with Hulda, Ester, and Ella to see the sights on Fifth Avenue, Rockefeller Center, the Empire State Building (although we did not get to go up to the top), and do a little window shopping. While in New York, Hulda and Ester got to see some more of this enormous city, go out to eat in restaurants, and stroll in Central Park with cousin Ella.

Our whole family also made a trip to Massachusetts to visit another cousin, Karl Kusik (Aunt Roosi's second son), and his family. When Estonia was still free, Karl had been the Consul General of Estonia in the US. However, in 1938, he was called back to Estonia for another Estonian government assignment—to be the First Secretary of Foreign Affairs—so he, his wife, Mary, and their two children, Lembit and Mairi, who were about my age, had moved to Tallinn. We had visited them there in their beautiful home and marveled at all their American toys. (When they left Estonia, Kaljo inherited Lembit's pedal car that you could sit in and pedal with your feet to make it go—white with red stripes! Pretty amazing in 1939.) However, when the communists overthrew our government and took over Estonia, Mary and the two children, being US citizens, were allowed to leave for America. It's a lengthy story of how marvelously, through a good deed that Karl had done while being the Consul General in New York, God made a way for him to get out of Estonia under such unbelievable circumstances.[4] All four family members were able to leave Estonia on the same ship, via Sweden, to the United States in September 1940. Karl was so stressed over all the interrogations he had encountered with the communists before he got out, that when they finally did arrive back in America, he wanted nothing more to do with politics. Instead, they bought a beautiful chicken farm in the midst of the rolling hills in Richmond, Massachusetts, not far from Boston.

With cousin Karl Kusik and family in Massachusetts

We had a wonderful visit in Massachusetts with cousin Karl. By now, they had two additional children, Edgar and Anne. We all piled into the back of Karl's pickup truck, and he drove us around their property. There was a creek and a little dam and the sights of the green hills were so picturesque. That evening, after a delicious chicken dinner that Mary prepared, they drove us to see Tanglewood, the nearby summer home of the Boston Symphony Orchestra.

Back in New York, we had enough time to bid all of our Eastern relatives good-bye and then, with cousin Erica accompanying our family, we boarded a train headed west.

Part of the first day and night on the train were spent heading from New York to Chicago. When we arrived in Chicago, Erica got us a taxi so we could change trains at a different railroad station where we were to continue our journey alone. It would have been very confusing for us by ourselves to handle all this in a strange and big city. Erica had become very dear to us by now and so with lots of hugging, she saw us to our train and then returned back to New York.

Our family traveled west on the Great Northern Empire Railway, on and on . . . for two days and nights through fields of wheat and corn, farms, wooded meadows, cities, towns, mountains, and miles and miles of prairies. By this time, we were getting very tired of sitting and eating mainly sandwiches, apples, and snacks brought along from New York (since we wanted to keep the little "food money" that our relatives had given us, instead of using it in the expensive dining car). Finally, we traveled along the wide Columbia River for several hours until we eventually arrived at our destination—Portland, Oregon.

At the Portland Union Railroad station we found our two uncles, Charlie and Walter, waiting for us. Although Papa had not seen them since he was a young boy, we recognized them from their pictures. After introductions and greetings, Mamma and we children got into Uncle Walter's beige 1937 Dodge while Papa rode in a neighbor's pickup with most of our suitcases. We three girls were in the back seat and Mamma and Kaljo were in front.

Our Big Move

As we left Portland, I guess Uncle Walter was so excited by our coming and by talking with us that he went right through a stop sign. Another car, although it came to almost a halt, hit us on our right side. This certainly didn't seem like a very good start for us, but at least the damage to the cars was minimal. After Uncle and the other driver did some talking, we rode on.

There was much to see as we drove across the Columbia River to Washington State. Uncle told us that this was the third largest river in the United States. We continued north through the town of Vancouver and then headed about fifteen miles east through little settlements, like Orchards, Brush Prairie, and Hockinson. Here we made a quick stop, and Uncle went into the Hockinson Co-Op store, picked up a few groceries and a bag full of fresh doughnuts.

As we drove on, the gravel road got narrower and narrower and we kept climbing higher and higher in the foothills of the Cascade Mountain Range. In the back seat we were whispering to each other, "Will we ever be able to find our way out from here again?" "Will we ever even be able to leave this place again?!" Finally, we made a turn to the left, shortly after that, a sharp curve to the right, and finally another right turn by mailbox number 248 – through a gateway into "THE FARM."

Chapter 11

The Farm

The Konsa Farm became our new home and a landmark for many, many years to come. This sixty-three-acre farm had been bought and established (as mentioned earlier) by my uncle Walter Konsa in 1908 when, as a young man, he had come here to live. At that time there were no real roads and the land was mostly filled with huge fir trees, some cedar, different kinds of deciduous trees, and lots of underbrush.

First he had built a small hut for his basic needs and started clearing the land. In the following years, he established a chicken farm and a six-acre Italian prune orchard, a farmhouse, and the needed buildings. At first, all the work was done by his bare hands, some basic tools, and the help of a horse. The nearest store and post office were about five miles away in Brush Prairie.

Uncle Walter's Farm

As years went by, more and more people settled in the area, many of them of Finnish descent. There were other Estonians, mostly in Portland thirty miles away and also in the Seattle area over 200 miles north.

Eventually Walter married an Estonian divorcee, Mary Beckman, who had one small son, Edward. Walter adopted the young boy and with Mary, raised him until he joined the US Army. Sometime in the past there had been a forest fire that had touched Uncle Walter's land as evidenced by burned-out and charred tree stumps visible on the hillside as well as on his property.

When our family arrived here at the beginning of June 1947, Papa was fifty-five, Mamma forty-six, Hulda seventeen, Ester sixteen, Kaljo eight, and I was thirteen years old. Uncle, who was sixty-two, had become a widower when his wife died more than two years earlier.

The Farm

As we entered the large cleared yard of the farm, on the right was an old one-story house. This, Uncle told us, was the "brooding house," used early each spring when baby chicks were brought here to keep them in a very warm room, heated by intensive electric heat to keep them cozy-warm until they grew bigger. Close to that house was a huge barn for cows and hay; across the yard on the left side were long chicken houses; next to those was the outhouse and a garage where we all got out of the car. The yard itself was overgrown with long grass. Dogs came running out barking at us; some of them seemed rather wild-looking.

With Uncle leading the way, we followed him to the "inner yard" separated by a hedge of pink roses. Next to the farmhouse under the windows were big blue hydrangeas and dark pink camellia bushes.

The Konsa Farmhouse—our new home

The two-story farmhouse was light green with a front screened-in porch. We entered a large kitchen with a round oak table and chairs, a wood-burning stove, refrigerator, sink, and yellow cabinets on the walls. The main floor, in addition to the kitchen, consisted of a living room, dining room, pantry, small hallway, and bathroom that included a sink, an old-fashioned bathtub and toilet—all with running water (as in the kitchen). We were actually amazed that all the water was piped into the house from a spring some distance away on the hillside. There was also central heating, with a wood-burning furnace in the cellar that piped the heat through heat ducts to the main floor.

On the second floor were four rooms. The first tiny room under the eave was to be mine—actually my own private room (a first in my life)! Kaljo was to share a room with Uncle; Ester and Hulda had a room with a dormer window down the hall; and Papa and Mamma's bedroom was at the end of the hallway. We had never before had this much room for living space!

After we had a meal, there was yet much to explore outside the house. With the deep grass all over the yard, there were many garden snakes that we had to watch out for, to keep from stepping on as we continued our tour of the farm. There was a kind of catch-all shed where firewood and some tools were kept, an area for a big green Oliver tractor, and some junk on the other side. Then we saw another big building that, at the time, was half empty, but where chickens were also usually kept. The whole farmland was on a hillside and from the top, the view was picturesque with rolling hills and wooded valleys, and farms here and there. At night one could see the glow of the skyline and lights of the city of Portland nearly thirty miles away.

On part of this hillside stood the prune orchard with trees planted so perfectly in rows that no matter where you looked from, they were lined up like tombstones in a military cemetery. There were also apple, plum, and cherry trees, a big walnut tree, and two Japanese cherry trees so laden with fruit that the branches hung to the ground. Parts of the land were just hayfields. A creek ran through one side of the land, and the farm animals could roam around there in a fenced-in area as well as near the barn. Well, with all this, you can be sure that there was more than enough work for all of us. And we had not yet toured the chicken houses.

So on our first day, it was then time to gather eggs. With wire baskets in hand, we all followed Uncle to the long chicken houses where several thousand white leghorn chickens seemed to be everywhere on the floor, by feeding pens along the outside wall, on their sleeping lofts, and in their nests, and that's where we found the eggs of course. As we walked from one chicken house to the other, our baskets filled up. There was also a feed room that connected the separate chicken houses where feed was kept in big sacks. From here, the feeding pens, as well as the drinking containers, needed to be filled with fresh water.

Then we brought the eggs to the cool cellar of the farmhouse. Here were several wooden crates and little stools by them where eggs had to be cleaned with a very fine sandpaper block and sorted according to size. This became the routine work for us each day, with hundreds of eggs to clean, sort, and stack in large crates.

Each week, Uncle drove to the co-op in Vancouver to market the eggs and bring back empty egg crates. This was the main source of livelihood and Uncle handled all of the money—we had none. In fact, we very seldom got to the store. Uncle brought a big sack of flour, a big sack of oatmeal, some canned pork and beans, sometimes some bacon, hamburger meat, and at times fresh doughnuts (besides staples such as sugar, salt, baking powder, etc.). We had eggs, milk, chickens, fruits, and we also started growing all kinds of vegetables ourselves on the farm and the following year, as he had in Estonia, Papa started keeping bees.

There were several cats on the farm. Most of them stayed around the barn and were wild. They lived by eating mice and got some milk each evening when uncle milked the cows. There were also a couple of dogs, Mongo and Bongo, that didn't come near the house. The friendly mother dog, Daisy, had one blue and one brown eye and was every shade of white, brown, black, and gray. When we asked Uncle what kind of dog she was, he said, "She's an American." Some days after we arrived on the farm Daisy had the cutest pups, a light beige one Uncle called Bingo and a black one with white front and paws we named Sulla.

Sunday on the Farm with our family

. . . And now we are farmers!

Ester and Mairy gathering eggs

The city of Portland is called the City of Roses and every June they organize a big Rose Parade. Each high school selects a princess from their school and out of all these girls, a queen to preside over the Rose Parade is chosen. Some Estonians from Portland took us to see this Rose Parade with many, many marching bands and beautiful floats decorated with all kinds of roses and other flowers. This was truly a sight to behold and we oohed and aahed as we stood on the sidewalk and watched. Popcorn vendors sold popcorn in small paper bags. Our hosts really wanted to treat us and so they bought us popcorn, which we had never ever eaten before. We tried to be polite and thanked them and tried to pretend that we liked it, but try as we might, we really didn't like it. Hulda was wearing a light overcoat with a lining that had a loose armhole seam . . . so we started quietly dropping the popcorn into her coat lining through her sleeve until we had the whole bagful pretty well hidden there. No sooner had we "eaten" that, when a new bag was bought for us! The result of this popcorn story was that when we got home and tasted it again, we discovered that we had gotten used to the taste and the more we ate, the better we liked it. For me, popcorn became one of my favorite snacks!

Uncles Walter and Charlie 1947

Each Sunday our Uncle Charlie came to visit us on the farm. He was really a dear man. He was married to an English lady and they had no children. Uncle Charlie owned a nice brick home and a barbershop in Portland. He was a very interesting man, well read and with a wide range of knowledge. One day he took Hulda and Ester shopping in Portland and bought them each a nice winter coat. He said there was no way that Mamma should continue for any length of time to be "just a farm-wife," but with her education and outgoing personality, she should be in some kind of sales or leadership position. He also said we children should all go on to universities since he saw such great potential in each of us. First, however, we were all to learn to speak English well.

One day Uncle Walter took us children to a first/second grade school teacher, Mrs. Barton, who lived nearby. Mrs. Barton gave us the children's reading book *Dick and Jane*. She started teaching us to read English: "Look. Dick," said Jane, "come, Dick, come. Jump, Spot, jump . . . etc.," so by the time school began our English vocabulary was obviously still very limited.

Uncle was a good-natured, good-humored, easygoing man with an almost bald head and a full moustache. When at home, he usually wore a faded blue Levi shirt and bib overalls and when outside, he put on a light straw hat. His place at the big round kitchen table was by one of the two windows next to the refrigerator, and after meals he always crossed his hands and laid his head down to take a little nap at the table, saying, "I've got to do this so the food won't think it's in a dog's stomach."

He was very active in community affairs, and he led in different campaigns whenever there was some good cause, like getting a fire station in Hockinson, or some measure that needed to be put on the voting ballot to benefit the county. Uncle was also active in the local Finnish Kalevi Lodge and was a director of the Washington Chicken Co-Op Association. Every so often he made trips to Bellingham for directors' meetings. He told us that some years ago during these long board meetings, he got headaches and some friends advised him that in order to get rid of his headaches, as others there smoked, he should also start smoking, even though he hadn't smoked all his life. So when we came to live with him, he smoked, something our family was not used to at all. But since it was his home, we had to endure that. Mamma often washed and bleached the white hand-crocheted trimmed curtains in the kitchen that were yellowed, especially by the window where Uncle always sat. (Many years later, he had an operation for some ailment and when he came home from the hospital, he had quit smoking "just like that" and said that since the doctors and nurses got his stomach all cleaned up and "washed out," he didn't want to dirty it up again.)

Uncle was a God-fearing man but not a "church-goer." In Hockinson, there was a Lutheran church and also a very small Community church next to the schoolhouse three miles away. Since none of us drove, we didn't attempt to go to church but had our own service, as we usually did under such circumstances.

Our round oak kitchen table became our altar for years to come, where we gathered for singing, Bible reading, and prayer, and now with Uncle joining us, we did this each evening and on Sunday mornings. Uncle too, had a good singing voice and loved to sing, especially some of the old hymns, like "In the Sweet By and By" (*"Püha auline inglite maa"*) that he had learned as a boy back home.

Estonian Picnic at The Farm 1947

On the Fourth of July, we had an Estonian potluck picnic on the farm with about sixty people from the

Portland and Seattle areas. This had already become a tradition for Uncle here while his wife was alive. Now Papa conducted a church service by leading in a hymn, Bible reading, a short message, and prayer before we ate. The people who came had emigrated from Estonia to the States mostly before or after the First World War, so they spoke Estonian mixed with lots of English words. We thought this sounded so weird. Afterwards, we girls sang, and they were awed listening to us sing patriotic and folk songs in pure, clear Estonian, and they wanted to hear more and more of our singing.

Hay-making time was a busy time. Uncle drove the tractor and Papa sat on the back hay-cutting machine that had previously been pulled by a horse. Even though now all this equipment was pulled by the tractor, somebody still needed to be on it. This was also the case with the hay raker in order to pull it up when you went around the corners, etc. When it was time to make small haystacks and then take the hay to the barn, the whole family helped. In later years when Ester and Hulda were gone and Papa attended to other work, I usually sat at the back of the equipment and later still, Kaljo did. Ester was the first one in our family to learn to drive the tractor, and after that Papa and I did as well for many different jobs.

That first summer, Uncle and Papa took on the project of building us a real Estonian sauna. The sauna was heated with wood, with a shower in the heat room, which made it very nice since there was no shower in the bathroom.

We had good American neighbors, Ernie and Mitzy Horne, living on the next farm. Their eldest son, Bob, was the same age as Kaljo and soon they were playing cowboys and Indians together. They also had a younger boy, Jimmy, and a girl named Patty (later a daughter, Katrin or "Kitten" was born). Ernie, the father, was a pleasant man who was always ready to help whenever there was a need.

Chapter 12

School Days ❧

In September, Hulda and Ester went to live with a very friendly Estonian lady in Portland, Alice Allik. Her very quiet husband, Oswald, worked at an Oregon coast lighthouse, so most of the time he was not home and they had no children of their own.

Alice helped Hulda and Ester to get work at Meier & Frank Co. Department Store downtown. They worked in the basement in the packing/wrapping department where they didn't need to know much English. Two evenings a week, however, they attended an English language class. On Saturday evenings they usually took the bus to Vancouver where Uncle picked them up and brought them home. Soon after they had started working and had come home for a Sunday, the Willamette River flooded and a section of Portland called Vanport was completely under water. Hulda and Ester couldn't get back to Portland for the work week for two days, until they were able to cross the Columbia River and the flooded area by a small water plane (a big first for them).

In September, it was also time for school to begin and since Americans couldn't pronounce our first names correctly, Kaljo and I began to use our middle names, Dave and Gloria. This way, at least we didn't have to spell our first names since we had to spell Konsa anyway. Dave went with his new friend Bob to Mrs. Billings' third grade class, even though he had barely finished first grade in Sweden in May. He blended right in and followed basically what Bob did and what Mrs. Billings wrote on the blackboard. I had to go to the fifth grade and felt so dumb next to all the ten- and eleven-year-old children in my class because by now I, at thirteen, looked more like a little lady. I usually told everyone I was a year younger than I actually was.

This was a small country grade school for the first through eighth grades in the community of Hockinson. The yellow school bus picked us up each morning by our mailbox and brought us back in the afternoon at 3:15. In each of the classrooms were two grades, so the fifth and sixth grades were together in my classroom and our teacher was Mrs. Rodgers. She was a very attractive tall, dark-haired lady with beautiful brown eyes. She wore bright red lipstick and had a friendly smile. She often wore a tailored gray suit and seemed to have the kids well under control.

School Days

Mrs. Rogers introduced me to the whole class. I understood her when she said "Gloria Konsa" and everyone clapped. I guess she explained that I had come from a foreign country and couldn't speak English. So when recess time came one girl came up to me and pointed to herself and said, "My name is Joyce Pietila." Then she pointed to her little purse and said, "purse, purse," which I tried to say after her, but it sure didn't sound anything like what she had said.

School for me was tough once again. I did my homework with an English-Estonian dictionary in one hand and a schoolbook in the other, trying to figure out what the lessons were all about. In school, it was also difficult because I did not have friends to run around with. During the first few days the girls were nice, but since girls that age do a lot of talking and since I couldn't join in to their chatter, they usually ran off in their own group. I then would spend recess and lunch hours either hiding behind a huge tree on the side of the schoolhouse where no one could see me or else inside in one of the bathroom stalls where I stayed for as long as I could.

At home after I had done my egg-cleaning chores and studies and had gone to bed, I often cried myself to sleep. I felt so dumb, so inferior to others in school, and I missed my friends in Sweden, longing to see them. It was always a joyous occasion when a letter arrived in the mail for me.

Prune-picking time came at the beginning of October. Besides Mamma, several neighbors came to pick prunes. Kaljo and I joined them after school and on Saturdays. With his tractor, Uncle brought the prune boxes on an open trailer and these were unloaded all over the orchard. The prunes had to be shaken off the trees, which Papa and Uncle did. After the boxes were filled, they were loaded on the trailer and then, at the end of the day, were taken to Vancouver by truck to a drying plant and were then distributed for selling.

In late October, word came from Uncle Charlie's wife that he had had a heart attack and died at age sixty-four! This was so very sad for us, since we had come to love and appreciate him and his wise counsel and insight. Papa conducted the funeral at the Elim Cemetery in Brush Prairie and soon after that his wife went back to live in England.

Our first Thanksgiving in America came. We had been studying about the meaning of Thanksgiving in school and learned about the first pilgrims to this new land and their struggles and hardships. Even though we had lots of chickens on the farm, Uncle bought us a turkey, as this was the American tradition. Mamma fixed a delicious Thanksgiving dinner with what she learned were the traditional Thanksgiving foods. Ester and Hulda had the day off work from Portland and joined us around the dining room table as we together gave thanks for the abundance and freedoms in America.

As before, when we were all together, we always liked to sing. As mentioned earlier, Uncle loved music, too, and agreed with us that we "needed" a piano. So just before Christmas he surprised us with a big gift—an old, used dark brown player-piano! This was really fun to play. We would put a paper roll with tiny holes in it into the piano, pedal with our feet, and the piano keys started moving by themselves, as the melodies they played were very advanced and sounded like an expert played them. Actually, they were pre-recorded by experts to do just that. The piano came with several of these rolls. But of course we could play this piano the regular way, and Hulda being the eldest, got to try it first by playing chords and we all joined by singing some familiar songs.

Before Christmas, Uncle and Kaljo went into the woods to chop down a Christmas tree and we found that Uncle's wife, Mary, had a box of ornaments and electric lights with which we decorated the big tree. We continued our Christmas customs with baking and cooking our traditional foods. It is also an Estonian custom to either sing, play, or recite a poem or Scripture verse before you get a present. In fact, we still do this with our children and grandchildren. It was really special to celebrate Christmas by singing and playing the old Estonian Christmas songs and carols around the piano. Uncle had never had a Christmas like this before and he thoroughly enjoyed it. But we never, ever forgot to pray for freedom in our land and for all our loved ones and our congregation in Estonia who we knew could not celebrate Christmas freely. We had not been able to write to them nor to get any word from them. They were truly "behind the iron curtain."

Mairy, Hulda, Ester, Kaljo. Our first Christmas in America

Chapter 13

Continued Life on The Farm

In 1948 a first for me was that by the end of March Uncle had found a piano teacher in Battle Ground and I started taking piano lessons. This was so wonderful and I practiced hard for each week's piano lesson. By the time I had my chores and homework done and got to the piano, Uncle was heading up to his room to sleep. He told me over and over again through the years that he had always wanted to go to sleep with someone playing music and singing for him and now his lifelong wish had been granted.

Each month Uncle received by mail a schedule for the local movie theater in Battle Ground with the upcoming films to be shown that month. Since he liked going to cowboy movies, he picked out the films he wanted to see and invited Kaljo and me to go with him. We had never been to a movie before, and Kaljo was so excited to actually see Western films of Roy Rogers and

Gene Autry. Roy Rogers became his favorite cowboy hero with his white hat, colorful cowboy shirts, guns with holsters, and a beautiful Palomino horse, Trigger. He wished he could get a Roy Rogers kind of hat, shirt, and boots. Over the next few years, he did receive his wish of a cowboy hat, shirt, and cap guns with holsters, but he never got the cowboy boots, which cost way too much.

I enjoyed hearing the singing of Roy Rogers and Dale Evans and the harmonious melodies of The Riders of the Purple Sage group in the films. For a time, some neighbors had a brown horse that they needed taking care of, which we did, but he wasn't much of a riding horse so we never really became "cowboys."

In Hockinson, it was basketball season. Every noon and at recess time, almost all of the kids rushed down to the cement-floor gym to practice and play basketball. During the P.E. or physical education class period, our fifth- and sixth-grade boys and girls usually formed two teams and each had a captain who, by taking turns, chose one by one, his or her team. Since I didn't know anything about playing basketball and a heavyset girl named Barbara couldn't run fast, she and I were always left standing last. This to me was so embarrassing that I vowed to myself that somehow I was going to learn to be so good at it that I would never have to be last again.

It rained a lot in the fall and winter, but when spring came I had already been hinting to Uncle and wondering if we could get a basketball and a hoop to put on the barn door. Eventually the day came when Uncle did just that. From then on, every chance I got, I was out there shooting baskets from every direction.

By the time the next school year came and when basketball was being played again, the same thing happened. Everyone was picked for the team except Barbara and me. We stood there and waited . . . and whichever team I got on, I managed to get the ball, dribble it down the floor, and hook a shot right into the basket—and everyone's mouth fell open! They couldn't believe what had happened with Gloria! You can be sure I was never left standing among the last ones after that again.

Grade school friends: Fern, Mairy (Gloria), & Barbara

My Father's Guiding Hand

The new year, 1949, brought a change in our family. Esther, who now spelled her name with an "h," the American way, started her junior year of high school. She had continued working through the whole year 1948, just so she could receive the $100 Christmas bonus that was given to all who had worked a year or more by Christmas. She had learned some English—from the English language classes and what she could learn while packing and wrapping boxes at Meier & Frank's department store. She had earned some money and had bought a few school clothes.

The nearest high school was seven miles away in a small town called Battle Ground. Esther took the school bus with us to Hockinson, and from there all the high school kids from around there took another school bus to Battle Ground. She had missed a year and half of school and with all the new circumstances, it was a big adjustment for her. At home, the English-Estonian dictionary was getting used by both of us. Hulda now continued alone with work and night classes in Portland and had made new friends, so she was doing quite well.

By now I had many friends in school since I had no trouble speaking everyday English. Fern Sakrison and Joyce Pietila, both of whose grandparents had originally emigrated from Finland, became my closest friends. On rare occasions, we spent nights at each other's houses. I was also on the softball team and enjoyed that as well. We had competitions between other grade schools in the area and our school excelled in both softball and basketball. Our school colors were blue and gold and during my last year at Hockinson I also got to be a cheerleader.

The following year when I started in the seventh grade, I wanted to "catch up" somewhat with my age group. The school principal, Mr. Tatman, taught seventh and eighth grades so he became my teacher. Uncle and Papa both came to the school to talk with him to ask if somehow I could do the two grades in one year, but the reason he didn't want me to graduate from the eighth grade in the spring was that he didn't want to lose me as the star basketball player. Our girls' basketball team was the champion in the whole league. But finally Mr. Tatman gave in and I did finish the Hockinson Grade School that June, 1950.

Performing in Hockinson: Sylvia, Shirley, Ruth, Joyce, and Gloria

Ice skating on the pond behind the farmhouse with the sauna to the right

Esther and I leaving for school

Hockinson School 7th and 8th grade class
(Gloria 2nd from right, 2nd row)

Grade 8 Graduation 1950

During my years in Hockinson Grade School, we had a music class where I learned many traditional American folksongs and outside of school I formed a little girls' singing group. We sometimes sang for different programs at the Finnish Kalevi Social Hall. I also sang solos there. The first solo I sang publicly in English was "Beautiful Dreamer" by Stephen Foster.

During my years of living on the farm, for a while I went to the Lutheran church in Hockinson since they had a choir and a youth group called Lutheran League. The youth group occasionally had great roller skating parties. I became a fairly good skater and every now and then also went to skate in Portland at a large roller skating rink.

During the summer, our youth group went on an outing to Mount St. Helens, a dormant volcanic mountain over 14,000 feet high that was covered with snow year round. This was about fifty miles from Hockinson (thirty-five miles by air). We took a sack lunch with us, had a picnic in a park area, and then took a hike into the cave inside the mountain. This was kind of spooky, yet it was something so different from what I had ever done before. Fifty years later, in 1980, Mt. St. Helens erupted, with volcanic ash spewing for hundreds of miles around!

Continued Life on The Farm

That fall, we finally got a telephone. It was a three-party line. Our phone number was TW(ining) 23708 or by dialing 892-3708. Mitzy, our neighbor lady, did a lot of talking, so sometimes it was hard for us to get the line or the line was busy when people tried to call us, but still it was good to finally have a telephone. We had not had a telephone since the time that the communists took away our phone in Ridala.

On Sunday afternoons, Kaljo and I used to listen to baseball games on the radio and we were big fans of the Portland Beavers baseball team. In 1950, we also got a black-and-white TV, and every Saturday night we watched the "Hit Parade" with all the new popular songs. My favorite songs at that time were "Harbor Lights" and "The Four Leaf Clover," but every week new songs came out and we learned them all.

We had wondered what had happened to our relative Volli Konsa, who had come to Estonia from Russia with his grandmother and her goat during the German occupation. We knew that at age fifteen he had enlisted in the Estonian unit of the German Air Force to serve against communists, but we had no idea if he was still even alive. Through the Red Cross and different channels, Papa finally made the contact and found that, sure enough, Volli had gotten first to Belgium and then to Germany with other troops and there he had married a German girl named Margot. In fact, by the time we learned this, they had a two-year-old son, Harry. We arranged for the whole family to immigrate to the States, and they came to live with us on the farm. They were with us until Volli was able to get work and rent an apartment in Portland.

During 1949 to 1952, there was a surge of Estonians immigrating to the USA and also to our area. These were displaced persons (DPs) or actually refugees who had gotten out of Estonia by ships or in some other way to Germany when their troops were retreating just before the Russian takeover in 1944. In Germany, they had been placed in DP camps, but by now they had gotten sponsors in America, many through Lutheran churches or individuals.

One of the first families with whom we became good friends, who had also come over through Germany, was the Mägi family. In Estonia, they came from the Island of Saaremaa. Their children were about our ages. Karin and Anne became my good friends, Rein and Kaljo became close buddies, and Esther and Martin went out together. Hulda also made new friends among Estonians in Portland.

Three other families also moved to Hockinson. The Annus family had three boys, Heino, Arvo, and Matti, who were around our ages. Their two older boys started attending Battle Ground High School, but the following year they moved to Portland. The second family was a lady, Laine, with her young son, Otto, and after some years she married her divorced sponsor, Franklin

Mattson. Third was the Luik family, who had one son, Rein, who started in the ninth grade with me at Battle Ground Junior High.

The Konsa Farm became a kind of "hangout place" for many of the Estonians living in the area. The whole place had taken on a beautiful "new face" that was different from how it had looked when we first arrived. Papa and Mamma had planted all kinds of flowers in the yard and the grass was always cut. Hulda, too, loved flowers and digging in the yard when she came home on weekends. The Estonian picnics continued to be held here every summer. In the big yard a volleyball net was set up, the youth played ball, the children played games and loved jumping on the hay in the barn, and the older people sat around and visited. Usually we, the younger people, also went swimming at Battle Ground Lake where the water was very cool, clear, and refreshing.

Besides the picnic times, people just dropped in to be out in the country, to take a real Estonian sauna, or to just visit our friendly family, who greeted them with open arms. They always got some free berries or apples or could buy fresh farm eggs for less than in stores. All this made for a lot of extra work for Mamma since she always baked something, like her high chiffon cake or apple or plum coffee cake to serve with coffee or punch. Other times she cooked bigger meals, depending on what time of the day people came.

Mamma was so fast with her hands and was such a hard worker. But by being the "people persons" that she and Papa were, their life was more varied than the dull everyday routine and hard farm work. Before people left, Papa always sent them off with a farewell prayer. Then during our evening prayer time, he prayed for them that somehow our living testimony and words would speak to their hearts and they would come to know Christ personally.

During those years Uncle wanted to clear more land to grow some oats for feeding the animals. In order to do that, he, Papa, and Kaljo cut down trees on two areas on the hillside and by using dynamite, cleared the old charred tree stumps left from the forest fires. Kaljo though that was quite exciting, especially seeing the tree stumps blown up with dynamite! Mamma still always sang as she worked in the kitchen or while doing chores. During fall or winter evenings when it got dark early and they heated the house with the big wood-burning central heating system in the cellar, Mamma brought fresh apples to the kitchen table where she cleaned and sliced them. Then she took the apples to the dining room where she placed them on a screened frame in a sectioned-off covered corner by the heat duct to dry. The apples then dried for several days till they were nicely brownish and crisp. Oh, how good Mamma's dried apples tasted! We would stick them in our pockets and munch on them as snacks, and Mamma now and then made fruit compote by adding dried prunes and raisins. This was also one of our traditional Christmas desserts when we ate it with whipped-cream topping.

The days were long for both Mamma and Papa with so much work, so Mamma usually fell asleep right away when the day was over. Papa, of course, was tired too, however, he wanted time to fill his spirit with reading, studying the Bible and writing, and at times he stayed up very, very late. He kept a short diary each day about the temperature, the day's visitors, happenings, correspondence, etc., and he often wrote in red pen, "Praise the Lord for all His goodness!" Often he went to bed in the wee hours of the morning and Mamma woke up and asked him if he was "coming or going" (coming to bed or getting up in the morning).

They never complained, but sometimes Papa joked that he had a "big congregation (of chickens) to preach to." Occasionally, whenever it was possible, he conducted Estonian church services in Portland at the YMCA. But with the education, talents, and experiences they both had, it really was sad that at a still relatively young age they could not use their gifts anymore in full-time service for the Lord.

Chapter 14

My Junior High and High School Years

Battle Ground Junior High and High School together were quite large, with over a thousand students from quite a wide rural area and the small town of Battle Ground. I enjoyed meeting many new kids and got involved in different activities and sports. Being in a college preparatory course, I had to take such courses as chemistry, algebra, geometry, physics, a foreign language, and others (besides the general course subjects), and for electives, I mostly took art and music. Spanish was the only foreign language offered and I enjoyed that, since the pronunciation is almost the same as in Estonian, which made it easier for me. Our Spanish teacher, Mrs. Ricker, often said to the class, "Listen to Gloria, how she pronounces the words, especially the r's and the l's."

During my senior year the class was given names of students in Spanish-speaking countries to have as pen pals. Since Papa had a small address book from Estonia with him with Uncle Leo's address in it, I wrote to my own half-cousin Susanna as my pen pal. They still lived in Buenos Aires, in the Spanish-speaking country of Argentina. I had never corresponded with her, but now with some knowledge of Spanish, I was glad when she wrote back and told me that she, too, was going to high school and what she liked and did. I tried to keep up with our correspondence, but after a few letters, I didn't hear back from her and we lost contact.

Lavonne Cone had already become my best friend in junior high and she continued to be that throughout my high school years. She was a very sensible Christian girl with light brown hair and a beautiful singing voice and she played the piano for the school choir. Our choir director was Mr. Peru and I really enjoyed that class. For Christmas we learned the "Hallelujah Chorus" from Handel's "Messiah" and it became a tradition to sing this at the end of every Christmas concert when Mr. Peru called all of the former choir members in the audience to come up and join in. In the choir we sang varied songs from musicals and Negro spirituals, as well as some classical and Latin pieces.

My best friend, Lavonne Cone, and I at our house

I got my driver's license the summer after I turned sixteen, although I had driven the tractor long before that. Papa, who had gotten his license before I got mine, mostly taught me. He was so patient, giving me lots of confidence. After I had had my license for only a few months, I was speeding down a country road with the old '37 Dodge doing nearly fifty miles per hour in a thirty-five mph zone. Of course, wouldn't you know it, from out of nowhere a policeman appeared and stopped me. I got my first ticket and had to pay a $10 fine.

By now, Esther had graduated from Battle Ground High and was attending Clark Junior College in Vancouver, Washington. She was very popular and became a homecoming princess her first year and the prom queen her second year of college. Hulda also took some courses at Clark College, but during the summers she continued working at Meier & Frank's. Esther worked for two and half summers between college years as a waitress. This she did with several college friends, at a very fine restaurant called Irland's, right by the lake in Lake Oswego, a suburb of Portland.

Skiing at Mt. Hood

During the winters I sometimes went skiing with friends from high school or with other friends at Mount Hood, Oregon. Thus far I had only cross-country

188

skied, but here it was downhill slalom, quite different from cross-country. One time two of my classmates, Ray, Bill and I drove to Mt. Hood for a day of skiing and most of the ride home, Bill and I harmonized in singing together. At times Clark College students went to ski at Mt. Hood and Esther allowed me to go along. This was really great, as I enjoyed skiing more and more and on the way there and back we sang a lot on the bus. The singing on school buses was always fun and brought back memories of all the times of going to and from away games both in Hockinson and Battle Ground schools.

In those days, the shoe style for high schoolers was two-toned saddle shoes and the best brand name was Armershaw, which made cream and light brown-colored flats. They were quite expensive, costing around $30, but I finally bought a pair in my junior year with my berry-picking money. These were worn with rolled-down bobby socks. Ankle-length coats and either straight or flared ankle-length skirts and all kinds of sweaters and blouses were "in."

On cold and rainy days we wore head scarves. No one was allowed to wear jeans or pants to school except when going on camping trips or during different sports when shorts or pedal pushers (now called capris) were worn. Almost all of the girls had fairly short hair with curled ends; some also had "poodle cuts" that were popular. The boys wore crew cuts or short hair. You were popular when you got a "letterman sweater," and you got awards and pins for different sports and offices to put on your sweater. Our school colors were black and orange and our mascot was a Bengal tiger. The students in Pep Club wore bright orange short-sleeved sweaters with black skirts and little orange beanie caps. I still have my black letterman sweater in mothballs, but my orange sweater and beanie have disappeared somewhere along the way.

Siblings Hulda, Ester, Mairy and Kaljo on the
front steps of our house

Hulda marries Einar Eistrat in Toronto 1951

In the summer of 1951, Hulda and Esther took the train to Toronto, Canada. At the same time while many Estonians from Germany had emigrated to the States, many from Sweden had emigrated mainly to Toronto and Vancouver, BC, as well as to other parts of Canada. The Canadian government welcomed the hard-working, industrious refugees from the Baltic countries with open arms. Among them was a young man, Einar Eistrat, whom Hulda had met in Nyköping before we left Sweden and who had been corresponding with her. By now he had proposed and was begging Hulda to come and marry him in Toronto.

Several hundred Estonians had organized the Estonian Baptist Church, and at that time there were six other different denominational Estonian churches, an Estonian society, Boys and Girl Scouts, all kinds of clubs and choirs and a once-a-week Estonian school in Toronto. So, to make a long story short, Esther came back alone and Hulda and Einar, or "Eino" for short, were married on August 11 at the Estonian Baptist Church.

With so many Estonians also coming to Vancouver, BC, there were probably close to a hundred or so Christians who formed an Estonian United Church (the name "United" was chosen since they came from different evangelical denominations in Estonia). The Lutheran church here, as in Toronto, was much bigger, since most Estonians were traditionally Lutheran.

Some of the Christians in Vancouver, BC, knew Papa and they invited him to come and preach there every so often. Esther and I also made several trips with him by train some weekends and we sang duets at the church. We three were always eagerly awaited guests.

A Christian family from Taebla (near Haapsalu), Evald and Salme Leps, with their daughter Maie, who was several years younger than I, had moved to Seattle. Evald attended Seattle Pacific College and was studying for the ministry. They had escaped from Estonia to Sweden and from there immigrated to the States. Salme was a good seamstress and was working at Penney's in its alteration department in Seattle. Soon Evald accepted a pastorate near us at Venesborg Covenant Church, and he and Maie moved there, while Salme continued to work in Seattle. Since Maie had no siblings, I became kind of like a big sister to her. I gave her piano lessons and she enjoyed singing by the piano with me even after her lesson was done.

The Leps family had some good friends in California and right after school was out, they took a vacation trip by car. Esther and I were invited to make the trip with their family, which we were very excited to do. It was a long, hot drive but very interesting.

One of our first stops was in Sacramento to see the California State Capitol. We could not believe that the weather could possibly be as hot as it was there! The thermometer showed 108 F (or well above 40 C)! There were palm trees and tropical flowers all around the capitol and the whole place looked very impressive. We drove to San Francisco to see more sights and then took an inland road further south.

We visited and stayed overnight with different Estonians in the San Jose area and in Fresno where we also saw thousands of acres of grape groves and fruit trees. Many of the superhighways were lined with colorful red, pink, and white oleander bushes for miles. The whole trip lasted nearly two weeks.

Our family was getting ready for getting our US citizenship. For me, it was not too difficult to learn all the history, the way a bill is passed, the different branches of our government, different presidents, and the present senators and congressmen, etc., since I had US History as a subject that year in high school. For Mamma and Papa, however, it took a lot of studying and memorizing. Even Esther and I had to go through all of this to make sure we knew all the details. The day was July 21, 1953, when we went to the Clark County Courthouse with shaking hearts for our examination. One by one, we were given a written as well as an oral test and each of us passed it with flying colors. Then we received a little individual American flag and our picture was taken for the local Vancouver, Washington, newspaper. We were certainly proud and grateful now to be Americans.

1954 was the year that we finally received our first letter from Estonia. After ten years of silence since our escape, Aunt Minda's daughter, Lehti, wrote. Apparently she had gotten our address from Papa's relatives still living in Estonia who, before the war and Russian takeover, had corresponded with our American relatives. We knew nothing of what had happened to either Papa's nor Mamma's side of our relatives, nor they of us or where we were by then. The only sign of life had been that one postcard that Esther had received in 1947 from our grandmother while we lived in Sweden and Papa had sent one without signing his name, but by his handwriting and postage stamp they knew we had made it to Sweden. We knew that any correspondence from outside the iron curtain could mean danger for them, so we did not write.

But Lehti took a chance, since Stalin had died in 1953 and from the information that leaked out, some of the big deportations seemed to be over in Estonia. Lehti wanted to let us know that both our grandfather (Rein Sünd) in 1948 and then grandmother (Marie) almost a year later, had died. Then she continued, . . . "You remember Juks (a nickname for her father). He got tired of just living in the old place, so he left his wife and headed east and she, in turn, went to the capital city to do construction work." We understood from reading between the lines that the communists had taken their large, beautiful farm, arrested him, and sent him to Siberia. Tädi Minda obviously was sent to Tallinn to do hard labor work. (Very much later, we heard some of the details, including that she was hauling heavy bricks with a wheelbarrow at clean-up sites after the Russians themselves had bombed the city during the winter of 1944 while we were still living in Estonia.)

In her letter, Lehti also indicated that by now she was married and her sister Milvi lived in another town,

Pärnu. Much later we found out that Arvi and Evi, the other two siblings, being just twelve and eight, were hiding at a neighbor's house when the arrest of their parents came in 1949. The two children (Arvi and Evi) were so frightened, but they knew where Lehti lived in Haapsalu and walked over ten kilometers to her house hand in hand, where they stayed until their mother had served her term as punishment for being a "capitalist." Juks was still serving his prison term in a hard labor camp in Siberia, being a double enemy of Russians—a private farmer and someone who had served in the Estonian National Reserves.

Our hearts went out to our loved ones and much prayer went up to our heavenly Father for protection and endurance for each of them, as well as our other relatives and all of our Estonian people.

At some point during those years when I lived on The Farm, our cousin John, who had first come to meet us in New York harbor, paid to have a small house built for his parents on one corner of the property of The Farm. So his parents, Papa's and Uncle Walter's sister Roosi and husband August Kusik, moved into the house. While they lived in that house, their children, John, Karl, and especially daughter Erica, visited them and us every now and then. My aunt and uncle became somewhat part of our family and walked over across the creek on the footpath to our house almost daily to get fresh milk from us or one of us would go and check to see if everything was okay with them.

After living near us for some years, Uncle August died in 1953. We couldn't leave Aunt all alone as she developed dementia, so a one-bedroom apartment was built, attached right to the farmhouse. The apartment was almost finished when Aunt Roosi passed away so she actually never got to live in it.

Chapter 15

Toronto

Now that Hulda was married and lived in Toronto, I longed to see her. She and Eino were living with his parents and they all worked during the week. Hulda wrote home and told us all about the different church activities and a summer camp they were planning for the first long weekend in August.

During the days in the summer, I worked the fields at different neighbors' farms, picking strawberries and raspberries to earn money. But the summer before my sophomore year, the last weekend in July, I took a train across the country all alone to Toronto, changing trains in Chicago and then traveling through the night on to Toronto. My round-trip ticket cost $123.

I got there just in time for the long weekend Family Camp, which was held near Lake Ontario on an Estonian's farm. We all stayed in tents and right away I made many new friends and even saw some old friends, like Ilme, Aasa, and Mati from Harg (Sweden). What a wonderful experience my time there was. There were several seminars and services, swimming times at the lake, campfire meetings at night with lots of singing and testimonies, messages each evening, and a church service on Sunday morning. It was sad when the camp ended on Monday afternoon.

I had made many friends, so during the week I got together with several of them. Ilme, Aasa, Mati, Viive, Guido, Kaljo and Lille took me to see different sites in the city by subway and we went swimming at Sunnyside Beach at Lake Ontario. It was so wonderful to also be with my dear sister Hulda. One Saturday, we went with a group from their church on an outing to Niagara Falls—it was awesome!

Leaving for Toronto, Canada

Tent #9 with new friends at camp

Estonian Baptist Family Camp near Toronto

Three sisters in Toronto

Two years later, Esther and I made the same trip to Toronto to see Hulda and my many friends, some of whom I had been corresponding with for the past years. By now, Hulda and Eino had their first child, a darling little boy named Allan. We planned it so we could again go to the church camp the first long weekend in August. Many of the activities were the same as before, only this time there were even more people and several families had come from the East Coast of the US as well.

On Sunday, August 3, 1953, the final evening of the campfire, there was lots of singing and I joined in, as I had known all these songs already in Estonia and had learned new ones on my previous visit to Toronto. There were several testimonies by different young people, and at the end an invitation was given for those who had never given their lives to Jesus Christ. Even though I never, ever doubted the power of prayer since I had seen many, many times in our lives how God had answered prayer, and I never doubted the Word of God, still I did not have a personal relationship with Jesus Christ, and I did not have the assurance of salvation that if Jesus came back for His own, I would go to heaven.

The guest speaker, Rev. Evald Mänd from Massachusetts, asked people who wanted to come to the Lord to come and kneel by the campfire. No one moved. I knew there were several kids from Christian homes who had never committed their lives to God. Even though I didn't even feel Christ speaking to my heart that night to make a commitment, as a pastor's kid I knew what to do to "open the way" for someone else to take that step. So I boldly got up from my seat, walked forward, and knelt by the fire. I started praying for the Lord to save me, then peeked up to see if anyone else had made a move. I saw one, two, three, several more at once coming and kneeling down next to me. Now I was earnestly praying, "Oh, Jesus, I want to be Your child, save me!"

A little while later, people around me were standing up and singing with joy in their hearts, but here I was,

I couldn't even cry . . . when all at once it was like the Holy Spirit said, "Just thank Me! I have done all to save you, I have gone to the cross and have died for you and paid the price for your sins, just believe and receive My salvation and thank Me!"

And as I started to thank Him, I couldn't stop. A joy and freedom filled me that I had never known before! "O thank You, Jesus! Thank You, Jesus!" was all I could say. I was born again!

Finally I got up and started singing with all the happy redeemed, young and old alike. Everyone was standing up and just praising and singing one song after another. There was revival in the camp. Hallelujah! So many "new babies" were born that night. No one wanted to go to sleep even though the hour by then was very late.

Finally, with several brand new believers' arms around each other, we made our way to the tent to get ready for bed. Once everyone was settled down, I got up and went outside our tent alone and looked up to the starry sky as I quietly said, "O God, You are so real to me! I worship You, I adore You, I love You!" A quietness and peace settled in my soul . . . a knowledge of being a "new creation" in Christ (see 2 Corinthians 5:17 NIV), and I almost wished that the sky would open up and Jesus would come and take me up to heaven! Finally back inside, I lay there so peacefully and rested.

The next morning was "camp as usual" and it was the last day of the camp, but for me, it was a brand new beginning in my new life with Jesus Christ. The sun was even brighter, the trees and the whole nature were greener, and there was a oneness of spirit with the people around me.

I saw Hulda coming from her and Eino's tent and ran over to her. We hugged each other, tears of joy filling our eyes. There were some more meetings that day and then the taking down of tents and cleaning up. Several of the families from the States were leaving that week to go back home, so there were good-byes with them. Others I would still see during the next couple of weeks in Toronto.

When we arrived home to Hulda's that night, I ran into the house to greet Eino's mom, who was waiting up for us with tea and goodies in the kitchen. I threw my arms around her and said, "I'm born again!" She responded by saying, "I could see that in your eyes the moment you walked in the door—your whole face was glowing!"

During the next week, Satan began attacking my assurance in Christ and he started whispering doubts into my soul. "You're so emotional . . . you're no different than before . . . this joy isn't going to last . . . you're just happy to be here . . . wait till you go back home, everything is the same. . . ."

I told Hulda about this and we prayed together. We knew that during the evening service on the coming Sunday night, Pastor Kaljo Raid would call all the young people up to give testimonies of what had happened to them at camp. Hulda said to me, "When everyone is called up, by faith, you go up too, and God will give you the words to say."

Well, when Sunday evening arrived, I did just that. When my turn came to speak, words just flowed out of my mouth so naturally that I was amazed when I shared with everyone that now I was a child of God and He had forgiven my sins and given me the assurance of salvation!

About a week later when Esther and I left Toronto Central Station in the evening, almost the entire youth group and many adults from the church came to send us off. We had been so happy together and now it was very hard to say goodbye. With many thoughts in my mind during the long train ride across the country returning home, even with Ester beside me, I was rather quiet. I tried to read my Bible, but my thoughts kept taking me back to all that had happened in the last few weeks. One thing I was so grateful for, though, was that I had peace in my heart. With Christian friends around me, I was baptized later in a small brook near Vancouver, BC by my Papa. I will never forget that day—it was as though the Holy Spirit descended upon me when Papa lifted me up from the baptismal water.

Chapter 16

Back on The Farm

I was very close to my parents. Throughout my life, there was always something I could learn from them, especially spiritually. I never heard them talking badly about other people or gossiping. They were always so grateful for everything and taught us to be likewise and to voice the same. They were so forgiving and taught us to ask and to forgive as well. They really lived and practiced what they "preached."

There were times when Mamma started to worry about different things, but when she had gone on for a while, Papa got almost stern with her and said, "That is enough. It's a sin for a Christian to worry about this or that. We can trust God to work things out and He will direct and guide us."

Then Mamma would realize that truly God does know all about our needs and she would say, "You're right" and soon she would again be humming a tune in her usual manner. As hard as the farm work was, sometimes when Mamma was really tired, I heard her sighing to herself, but I didn't hear my parents complaining or murmuring.

I could always pour out my heart to Papa since he understood and encouraged me, and even when I was already grown up and gone from home, whenever I came back to The Farm, I would go and sit on his lap and ask, "Papa, *kas ma olen pai*?" (Papa, am I good/sweet/well pleasing? There is actually no direct translation in English for the word *pai*.) Papa would answer back and say, "*Mairy-kene, jah, sa oled pai*." (Mairy dear, precious one, yes, you are *pai*. Here we have another Estonian word or actually a word ending that has no direct translation into English. "*Kene*" added to the end of a noun or adjective is a term of endearment; it's like adding "precious one," "dearest," or "little one" to the noun or adjective.)

When after our evening prayers Uncle and Mamma had both gone to bed, Papa and I would sometimes sit up and discuss personal matters, spiritual things, or other times even politics. As it got late, Papa would say, "Now, let's gather our thoughts and think about heavenly things; God wants us to go to sleep with Him on our minds." Papa then led in a short prayer asking that Jesus would cleanse our hearts and purify us to be ready to meet Him if He should come that very night. All such things, and many other godly things that I learned from my parents, helped me to grow in my spiritual life, for which I am forever grateful.

For a while we attended the little Community church in Hockinson that at the time had a good minister and where Papa and I sang in a choir of about ten to twelve people. Even though it was further away, now and then in my last year of high school I started going to the Brush Prairie Baptist Church where some of my high school friends attended.

I continued taking piano lessons and for a while took voice lessons. At the same time, I became a piano teacher to some of our neighborhood children as a way to pay for my own piano and voice lessons.

Dave (Kaljo) and I in front of the "bee house"
at The Farm, c. 1953

Our three April birthday men" Uncle Walter,
Kaljo and Papa, 1953

Summer at The Farm

Mamma, Papa, Mairy and Kaljo (Dave), winter at home 1954

Estonian National Costume

My Father's Guiding Hand

My last year of high school began with many activities and studies. During the second semester while playing volleyball against another team, I spiked the ball, making the point for our team, but I got a compound fracture in the forefinger of my right hand. I was taking typing that semester, a class that I thoroughly enjoyed because Miss Smith always played music while we typed so we could keep our typing consistent with the rhythm. She walked with a cane, but now and then she forgot about her cane and proceeded to walk just fine without it.

That fracture put an end to both my typing class and to my volleyball playing for the year. God had given me very good health, and I had perfect attendance all through my junior high and high school years. So even with my painful finger, I couldn't miss a day of school.

Uncle bought a light cream and navy colored '53 Dodge, since the old car by then was in very poor condition. But he let me drive the old '37 Dodge to go to various after-school ball games and other activities unless I had a date or got a ride with someone. It was a great school year. Lavonne, my best friend, and I often talked about what we would do after graduation. We both planned to go to college and then maybe marry a minister or be a missionary. Even though none of the guys I was friends with were planning to study for the ministry, yet somehow both she and I just knew that God would lead us to some type of Christian work. (Lavonne graduated from Northwest Christian University in Eugene, Oregon, where she met her husband, Tim Kribs, who became a minister, and they pastored different churches for many years until retirement.)

Life at home was much the same. Esther was now attending Western Washington College of Education in Bellingham, Washington, and studying to be a schoolteacher. Our brother Dave was in the ninth grade, and we were quite close and rode the school bus together to Battle Ground. Papa, Mamma, and Uncle worked as hard as ever, and with so much homework and school activities, we didn't help much.

High school graduation came with final exams and also the associated activities. We got our Bengals (year books) where next to my picture of the graduating class was printed, "Gloria Konsa . . . Mairy is a cute little blonde who is always full of pep. Her hobbies are art and skiing." I had been very active in high school on all kinds of committees, and I was Home Room Secretary one year, Home Room Treasurer another year, Student Body Vice President, high school Girls' League Secretary, Student Council representative, and I participated in style shows, girls' intramural sports, and the Tigerettes (Pep Club). I was on the Honor Roll for three years and in Honor Society, as well as singing in the choir, being Chairman of the rally committee, and more.

With senior year ending, there were more activities, such as the Senior Tea at Mrs. Engelman's, the Girls' League Camping trip, which was especially fun at Lewisville Park, and swimming at Battle Ground Lake when the water was still too cold—but who would admit that you were not brave enough to jump in to swim? And then, the graduation night itself.

It was sad to say good-bye to all the many friends with whom I had shared so many good times and fun. I was definitely no longer the shy girl who started out at Hockinson Grade School not speaking any English.

Girls League camping trip, from top: Lavonne, Lillian, Gloria, Bonnie, Trudy

Friends at Battle Ground Lake: Shirley, Gloria, Elaine, Nola

Gloria wearing her Battle
Ground High School
letterman's sweater

The High School Graduate
Mairy Gloria Konsa

Chapter 17

College Life ❧

For the summer months, I got a job at Meier & Frank's department store in the advertising department. In the fall when the school year began, I enrolled at Linfield College (a liberal arts college with a Baptist background) in McMinnville, Oregon.

McMinnville is a college town about seventy miles from The Farm. It has a beautiful campus with large oak trees and red brick ivy-covered buildings. I was assigned to Failing Hall girls' dormitory house in a second-floor corner room with two windows. My roommate was Pat Knudsen from Gresham, Oregon. Pat was a fun roommate, but she definitely didn't keep her part of the room clean and I had to cross it to get to my side of the room. I was always used to keeping all my things orderly and this frustrated me. Pat usually didn't study in our room, so I did a lot of studying there.

My college tuition at Linfield cost $240 per semester (x 2 semesters = $480) and room and board was $260 (x 2 = $525), so altogether it was $1,005. Due to the fact that Papa was an ordained Baptist minister, I got $100 off each semester, which made my school year cost $805. No one had given me advice that I could apply for either a partial or a full scholarship.

My classes were challenging and there was always more than enough homework. I majored in art, thinking of perhaps getting into interior design. My art teacher was fantastic. The psychology class was interesting, yet often I found myself drawing caricatures of my professor, Mr. Pistor, since he had a perfect nose for caricatures that was quite large and curved a certain way. He had a habit of walking around the room while lecturing and one time when I had just sketched his profile, he walked right by my desk and glanced down at my paper. I tried to cover it up, but he said, "Well, what have we here?" But then he added with a big grin on his face, "Actually that's a good resemblance of me!"

I did well in all my classes and enjoyed the professors, each in their own way. Everyone was required to take a class on the Life of Jesus during freshman year, consisting of the four Gospels, and I was grateful for that. Once a week we had chapel with some quiet meditation, singing, and mostly various upper classmen or professors speaking. After classes, I was on the women's field hockey team where sometimes the competition against other colleges became quite fierce.

College Life

Dorm life was fun. Across the hall from us was a girl from South Korea named Phibe Kim You Ja and her roommate Joan Henderson; next door were Pat Berg, who had a beautiful soprano voice, and Bunny Anderson, with a good sense of humor; down the hall were several girls who became good friends, like Claudia Verdieck, with whom we still exchange notes and Christmas cards; and her roommate, Gail Blush.

Every week we gathered with the whole dorm in our pajamas and robes on the main floor large, elegant living room. Here Mrs. Eva Mallory, our house mother, a gracious Christian lady, gave us some house rules, asked for questions, and led in a devotional and prayer. At the close, we all sang, "Good night, my God is watching o'er you. Good night, His mercies go before you. Good night, and we'll be praying for you. So good night, may God bless you! – Good night!" We also decorated this lovely room for our Christmas party and gatherings for different occasions. On Sundays, some of us went to the First Baptist Church morning service in downtown McMinnville; other times we attended concerts there.

Several foreign students attended Linfield and Dr. Colena Anderson was our advisor. One time she arranged an overnight trip for us to Astoria, Oregon, where each of us spoke at a city-wide Thanksgiving program at the Armory to benefit the "Share Our Surplus with the Hungry" Program. There were nearly 1,000 people present. Of course, I had given speeches before in speech class and had made campaign speeches in high school, but not like this. This was the first time I actually spoke about the horrors of communism and our escape and then sang a solo with one of the verses in Estonian.

At Linfield, there were also football and basketball games; dorm birthday parties; walks on Cozine Lane across a hanging bridge; the college President and Mrs. Dillon's teas and open house; the Christmas candlelight procession; the light opera, "Hansel and Gretel," where I had a part and sang as one of the gingerbread men, which was really enjoyable.

I didn't get home to The Farm very often, except for holidays when I took a bus to Portland, then to Vancouver, Washington, where Papa or Uncle picked me up.

With my college roommate, Pat Knudsen

Birthday party in the college dorm

Linfield College Girls Field Hockey Team
(Gloria, 2nd from right, front row)

I (front) with dorm friends, among others,
Claudia Verdieck, sitting in the back.

Linfield College Choir, Spring Tour 1955
(Gloria, center)

College Life

One of the best times of my college life was the spring tour of our choir by bus to California. We sang in many different churches, schools, and service clubs along the way through Oregon and as far south as San Francisco. Each place where we gave a concert, we stayed in different homes, but we also stopped to see various tourist sites, like the Golden Gate Bridge, the Cliff House, Mission Delores, Chinatown, the Fairyland, and the Berkeley Divinity School and University of California campus in the Bay area. The choir members became close friends and just singing together was a marvelous experience. Mrs. Elliot, our choir director, led us in closing each concert with a beautiful arrangement of the benediction, "The Lord bless thee and keep thee."

Chapter 18

A New Chapter in My Life

During Easter break when I was home from college, my whole life took a new and different turn. Esther was also home for Easter from teaching school in Seattle, and Kaljo was going to high school.

It was already close to 11:00 p.m. on Good Friday evening when the telephone rang. Mamma went to answer it in the kitchen and explained to whoever was on the other end, "No, Victor Konsa is not home. He went to Vancouver BC to preach for the Easter holidays and won't be back until next week . . . Well yes, of course you can come here . . . where exactly are you? . . . At this time of night, you would never find your way out here . . . But tell you what. Take the Orchard's Road West and since everything else is dark this time of the night, why don't you drive as far as Orchard's Tavern on the right side of the road? I'm sure lights will be on there. Just wait there and I'll send the kids to meet you!"

"Who was *that*?" I asked. Mamma explained that a young man, Endel Meiusi from Los Angeles whom Papa had met when he was down there for some meetings, would be waiting by Orchard's Tavern. "You better go and meet him."

"Yikes! I'm not going alone." So I got Esther to go with me, but she said, "No, we better take Dave with us because it's kind of funny for two girls to go and meet him!" Dave was just ready to go to bed, but we managed to get him to come along.

When we had driven approximately ten miles to Orchard's Tavern, sure enough, here was a little navy-blue-and-white Nash Rambler with a California license plate waiting, and out walked Endel Meiusi. None of us got out of our car, so finally I said, "Okay, you chickens, I'll go and meet him."

I got out, wearing my white Linfield sweatshirt and blue pedal pushers, and said, "Hello, I'm Mairy Konsa." Endel followed us home to the farm in his car (there was hardly any traffic by what was by then nearing midnight). Meanwhile, Mamma had made a bed on the living room pull-out couch and had hot tea and sandwiches ready for him.

Endel was a twenty-two-year-old, tall, dark, and handsome young man with wavy brown hair and blue eyes. With his family, he had escaped from Estonia in

1944 in a little fishing boat to Sweden some months earlier than we had. They had lived in Uppsala, Sweden, for five years and then immigrated to Australia where his parents were still living.

Endel had received a scholarship from Life Bible College at Angeles Temple, Los Angeles, to come and study for the ministry in the States. On weekends, he was often out speaking for Youth for Christ, which he was doing now as he was scheduled to speak that Saturday night in Portland. He had left his two college friends in Roseburg, Oregon, on the way here and thought he would take up Pastor Konsa's invitation to "visit him anytime he was near Portland."

On Saturday morning Endel had to drive back to Portland to meet with some Youth for Christ leaders so Esther and I went along to go shopping downtown. Meanwhile, she and I ran into a couple of our Estonian friends, Martin and Heino, who took us out for lunch and we weren't anxious at all to see Endel. Later he picked us up as planned and the three of us went to the Youth for Christ rally. Here the huge auditorium where Endel was to be the speaker was packed with youth. After a lot of music and singing of choruses, he preached quite a message and at the end gave an invitation to receive Christ. Many young people went forward to make that decision and to pray.

Meeting Endel, April 1955, with Evald Leps,
Esther and Maie Leps

On Easter Sunday morning we went to the nearby Venesburg Covenant Church that our good friend Rev. Evald Leps was pastoring. Afterwards he and his daughter Maie joined us for dinner on The Farm. In the afternoon, Esther left for Seattle, our visitors went back to their home, Kaljo hurried off to be with some friends, and after I helped Mamma with the dishes, Endel and I were kind of left with nothing to do. So instead of Endel leaving for California, he asked me to come with him to visit a church in Portland that he had wanted to see. It was too early to go there for the evening service, so we drove to the city to see some sites and to visit the famous Portland Rose Garden, then went to a drive-in for some hamburgers and finally to the evening service.

A New Chapter in My Life

As everyone was standing and singing "Blessed Assurance" and Endel was holding up the hymnal for me, it was as though God said to me, "Here is your husband!"

Endel drove me back to The Farm and on the way jokingly said that he'd rather take me to Las Vegas (where one can get married without a waiting period). Before he left that night to drive back to Los Angeles, he made sure he had my college address.

Back in Linfield, every time a letter came from Endel, the other girls (my roomie and the two girls next door who shared our mailbox) were always taking my letters and saying, "You've got to let us read it first!"

Each time I hoped that he wouldn't write in English. Luckily, most of the time he wrote either in Estonian or Swedish, even though I hardly understood some of the "love language" in Swedish.

By the time the school year ended, Endel had been writing me and asking me to come and visit him in Los Angeles. I decided to go for a few days before starting my summer job. My roommate, Pat, and I took a Greyhound bus to Los Angeles (L.A.) where she had an aunt in the area whom she came to visit. Endel met our bus and took me to the home of a dear elderly Christian lady, Johanna Paes, whom Papa had known already in Estonia. She was glad to have me come as planned and stay with her during my visit.

I had arrived in L.A. on a Friday afternoon and after a brief visit with Johanna, spent the rest of the day and Saturday with Endel. Saturday evening, he drove me way up beyond the clouds to the Hollywood Hills and there, with the view of thousands of city lights flickering below, under starry skies and a full moon above, proposed to me!

This for me was all too sudden! I sat there for what seemed a long time, quietly praying before saying anything. Even though my heart was beating fast, there was complete peace that this was of God and I finally accepted his proposal. We called Papa and Mamma and he officially asked Papa for my hand in marriage.

While going to college in L.A., Endel had pioneered and was pastoring a little Estonian congregation that Papa had visited earlier. Several people had come to the Lord and joined this congregation so there were about fifteen to twenty people attending.

The next morning in church (after his proposal to me), Endel had me play the piano to accompany the congregational singing, sing a couple solos, and share a testimony. After he had preached, his assistant made the announcement that Endel Meiusi and Mairy Konsa were engaged! Spontaneously one of the ladies jumped up and said out loud, "Hallelujah! Praise God! Our prayers have been answered!"

Endel was renting a room with a small kitchen not far from his college and asked if I would cook him a meal there. So using my cooking ability after shopping together, I cooked him a good Estonian meal of potatoes, ground-beef cutlets, gravy, carrots, and cucumber salad with dill and sour cream.

He had thought while we shopped that he'd better buy a bottle of catsup in case my cooking turned out so bad that he would have to pour lots of catsup on to eat it. Well, he forgot all about his catsup and later that evening we sat in his tiny kitchen, eating the leftover cold potatoes while dipping them in a tin can of spiced anchovy liquid that he had in his refrigerator.

Suddenly he looked at me so romantically and said, "You know, Mairy, I could never marry an American. They would never enjoy a meal like this with me."

One of the wonderful things about being with him was that we always prayed together.

Endel had worked hard hauling manure at a landscaping firm after classes to earn enough money to buy me a small diamond engagement ring that I wore when he put me on the bus and kissed me good-bye.

Back in Portland, I went to work at Meier & Frank's again, this time selling in the notions department. Our relatives, Volli and Margot, who by then had bought a house in Portland, allowed me to stay with them while I worked there. When school was out for Endel, he drove up to The Farm on his way to Vancouver, BC. There he was to work during the summer at the Lepik Construction Company owned by his two uncles, Paul and William (Villi) Lepik. It was so special to see him again, even for just the weekend, as we were so in love.

Endel and his Nash Rambler in California

Mairy – Engaged! In June

Chapter 19

Marriage

It was rather outrageous to think about marriage so soon, especially since we were both still in college and had no money. Logically, it didn't make any sense, but I knew being married to Endel, somehow with God being the head of our home, we would make it. He was so positive and nothing seemed unconquerable to him. Still I prayed and prayed, but there was such peace in my heart that when Endel wanted to set the date for our wedding for August 20, I started planning for that day.

I had to have a wedding dress! Hulda sent me her wedding dress and the headpiece. The dress had to be partly re-sewn. Our good friend Helena Mägi altered it and I made a new veil. My grade school-through high school friend Fern, as well as my college roommate, Pat, and also Margot Konsa (with whom I stayed that summer in Portland) gave me wedding showers with all kinds of household items as gifts.

There was a lot to plan and some of it was especially hard, since the wedding was to be in Vancouver, BC, Canada. Many of Endel's relatives, who had also escaped from the Russians to Sweden and then immigrated to Vancouver by that time, wouldn't otherwise be able to attend our wedding.

The weekend of August 11-14, Endel drove down to The Farm. I was to leave work earlier and meet him by the Vancouver, Washington, courthouse to obtain the legal papers for our marriage license. Early that morning as I was driving towards town from The Farm, there was a slight drizzle and the roads were wet. I saw a car in front of me starting to turn to the right to a side road. Instead of completing the turn to the right, the driver started turning his car around in the middle of the road! In order for me not to hit him, I turned far left, but with the wet gravel, my car flew on and then landed in a ditch that crossed under the road with a few inches of water in it. As I was "flying," I so vividly remember yelling out, "Jesus, I'm coming home!"

The next moment, I was lying sideways in the ditch with the car on its side, looking up at the passenger's side door! It seemed like an eternity as my mind raced from one thought to another. *Oh, I'm still alive on earth! Is this some kind of sign that our life will be very full of trials and testings? Am I making a mistake in marrying Endel? Am I hurt? Will I be an invalid? Oh, no, how will I even get out of here?*

Then a young man pulled open my car door. "Help, I can't get up!" I yelled. He started pulling me up and out of the car. I vaguely seemed to recognize him as an upper classman from Battle Ground High School. He and his sister were saying they were really sorry about what had happened, that he wasn't even aware that there was another car following him when he started making the U-turn on the road. His sister then ran to a near-by neighbor's house to call a tow truck. Time was ticking away. I needed to hurry to get to Portland for work, but this wasn't about to happen.

After a while, the tow truck came, pulled out my muddy car, and took it for repairs. To my amazement, the damage wasn't quite as bad as I had thought it would be, but of course the fenders and doors had to be fixed. The motor was fine as well as everything else under the hood. I guess I was more worried about Uncle's car than myself. I moved my arms, legs, my whole body, and didn't feel any kind of pain!

The young man drove me back to The Farm and later that day Endel and I drove together in his car to the Vancouver Courthouse to register and get the marriage license forms. We also went to the police station to report the accident. The police officer shook his head in amazement and said I could have been killed if I hadn't thought so quickly and turned to the far left. I was praying, "God, You must have something for us to do together, not to have taken me home yet when I so vividly remember expecting to fly into the arms of Jesus!"

That Sunday, August 14, 1955, after the morning service at Brush Prairie Baptist Church, Reverend Melvin Chapman legally married Endel and me as husband and wife. Our church wedding—what we really considered our wedding—was to follow six days later in Canada.

The following week there was still much to do, although I had already resigned from work at Meier & Frank's, the wedding invitations had been sent out about a month earlier, and our printed napkins were at hand. My dress was ready and Esther, who was to be my maid of honor, was to wear a light blue dress that she had worn to a girlfriend's wedding as a bridesmaid.

During that week, Endel, Esther, and I drove to Vancouver, BC together. At the Canadian border crossing, the border guard asked, "What is the purpose for your visit?" To which Endel responded, "We're on our honeymoon" and showed him our marriage license as well as Esther's and my US citizenship papers.

To this, the border guard asked, "Who is she?" pointing to Esther in the back seat. Endel, being a bit nervous, answered, "She's a school teacher!" Well, to make this story a little shorter, Endel had to get out of the car and go inside to show his own temporary student visa from Australia and do some explaining about what was going on, but eventually we were all let into the country.

Esther and I stayed with a good friend, a widow, Linda Vokksepp, in Vancouver, BC. She had two teenage children, Toivo and Tiiu. Esther and I slept on their front room couch. Endel of course was staying with his uncles for the summer.

Here we still had to prepare for the Saturday evening wedding, which was to take place at the Grandview Baptist Church on First Avenue where the Estonian congregation met every Sunday at 1:00 p.m. Endel drove Esther and me to the florist shop to order flowers for bouquets and decorations and to the bakery for the wedding cake. The Estonian ladies were preparing a dinner and coffee for the reception.

August 20, 1955 arrived. It was a beautiful cloudless, sunny day. Papa, Mamma, Kaljo, Uncle Walter, and my two cousins, John and Karl Kusik, arrived for the wedding from the States. Also my college friend, Claudia Veirdick, my roommate, Pat Knudsen, and her mother from Portland came, as well as the Leps family. The rest of the wedding guests were all Estonians from the

Vancouver area with the exception of the local Canadian pastor and his wife.

Esther helped me get dressed and ready and when Endel came to pick me up at Vokksepps', he just gasped! He thought I looked so beautiful! To me, he looked most handsome and dashing. At the church, everything was ready. Endel and his Uncle Villi, who was our best man, were dressed in formal white jackets and black pants and our flower girl, Lehti Ägi, was dressed in a pretty white dress with pale blue and pink flowers on it.

The wedding was a combined Estonian and American style ceremony, with the organ playing and Papa, the preacher, standing in front of the church. Esther and Villi walked in first, followed by the flower girl. Then the people rose and Endel and I, arm in arm, walked down the aisle. Papa preached a meaningful wedding sermon and besides some other music and songs, the choir sang:

"Where you go I will go, and where you stay I will stay. Your people will be my people and your God, my God. Where you die I will die. . . ." (NIV) Based on Ruth 1:16-17 from the Bible.

(In Estonian):

"Kus poole sina lähed, ka sinna lähen ma
Ja kuhu jääda tahad, ma tahan jääda ka.
See rahvas kes on sinu, on minu rahvas ka.

Marriage

Su Jumal, on ka minu, ja Õnnistegija
Siin võib meid lahutada vaid surm, ei keegi muu.
Truu Issand tunneb seda, et see mu kindel nõu."

After the laying on of hands by Papa while we knelt in prayer, he pronounced us husband and wife: Mr. and Mrs. Endel and Mairy Gloria Meiusi!

The downstairs reception/dinner at the church fellowship hall was full of long tables with white tablecloths and was filled with an abundance of food for the sit-down dinner, followed by all kinds of home-baked goodies and the wedding cake. There were speeches and music and it lasted a long time. Finally, we had to open our wedding gifts. Among them were some smaller and bigger presents, but the biggest gift was an album filled with cash gifts from most of the people from the church. Then, as Endel and I were going up the stairs, all the young ladies gathered around to catch my bouquet of pink roses as I threw it backwards.

Finally, with all kinds of cans and bells tied to our back bumper, everyone cheered us off. We spent the night in a nearby motel, since the next day at 1:00 p.m. we had to be back at the church as Endel had to preach at the Estonian church service!

Our wedding, August 20, 1955 (maid of honor:
Ester and best man: Villi Lepik in the background)

The newlyweds

A day later, Endel and I drove the approximately 350 miles to The Farm where the rest of the family had already arrived. Here we packed all our belongings on a small open trailer that we had bought in Portland. It was now time to say goodbye and to leave my family, The Farm, my home, and the life that had been familiar to me for the last eight years in America. With arms around each other and tears flowing from our eyes, Papa led us once again in prayer for God to lead our journey to California, to lead and guide our lives on life's journey together, for us to be a blessing to each other and to all whose lives we touch.

It was time to begin our honeymoon trip down Coastal Hwy. #101 to Southern California where we would both continue our college educations and start living our married life!

Ready to leave the Farm with all our belongings to embark on our new life together

Little did I know what an adventuresome life awaited me with Endel at my side—even going back to Estonia (as this story began)—with my heavenly Father's hand guiding us.

The End

(To be continued in Volume II,
Our Father's Guiding Hand)

Endnotes

1. Although it was part of Germany at the time, Bahnau is currently part of Poland right near the Russian border. Heilingenbeil is now part of Russia in the Kaliningrad Oblast and has been renamed Mamonovo. It is located about thirty miles southwest of Kaliningrad, which was called Köeningsberg at the time. During World War II, the school was destroyed. Information taken from *Das Tat Gott (in English: God Does It)*, published by Bahnau Mission School's Bookstore, Unterweissbach, Wurttemberg, Germany, 1956.

2. http://estonia.eu/about-estonia/history/estonias-history.html

3. There were not very many Jews in Estonia so the impact of the Nazis against the Jews was not felt as much in our corner of Europe, although later we found out that most who were there were killed.

4. Karl's story, "Passport From Hell," was accepted for their $25,000 First Person award by *Readers Digest,* however, to accept the money he would have had to disclose the names of people still living in Estonia. Karl chose not to accept the money as revealing certain names would most certainly have compromised the safety of certain individuals still in Estonia as it was at that time still occupied by the Soviet Union. The story was written up in an Estonian language publication in Toronto, Canada, but without revealing the identities of those individuals whose safety would have been at risk.

Addendum ✑

Names/dates/descriptions of immediate relatives mentioned in this book

My father's side of the family:

Peter Konsa (+/-1825) (my great-grandfather), father's side; married:

Amalia (my great-grandmother), They had four sons and one daughter

Hendrik Konsa (1849-1898, my grandfather) was their second son. Hendrik married:

Maria "Mari" Maaser (1852-1919, my grandmother), father's side. Maria's father's name was:

Hans Maaser (my great-grandfather), mother's side, wife's name unknown. They had nine children and my grandmother was the youngest.

My grandparents, Hendrik and Maria Konsa, had ten children (listed as numbers 1-10); the next (my)

generation is marked by 01, etc. and their children also mentioned in this book are marked by 001.

1 Gustav Johannes (1869-1881) died at age twelve of some kind of illness.

2 Emilie "Miili" (1870-1945), married Peter Narustrang. They had three children; stayed in Russia; owned a business until it was confiscated by the communists.

3 Alexander (1873-1945), was a businessman; farmer by Lake Kärnu. His first wife Helene (Maasing) died, giving birth to twin girls of whom one died, and the other lived:

01 Helen "musi tädi," lived 12/8/1902-11/6/2000. She immigrated to New York in 1925. Married William (Bill) Kerson; they moved to Portland in 1965; later to Florida where she died at age ninety-eight. No children.

Alexander married his second wife, Minna (Luik), in 1907. They had two girls:

02 Olga "Olli" (07/16/1908-1952), married Osvald Karp. Both were deported. Olli died in a prison camp under Stalin's regime and Osvald died in a Siberian slave camp; they had two children:

001 Heikki (08/12/1930-09/4/1953), was twelve years old and staying with grandparents when his parents were arrested; never married; buried in Tallinn.

002 Pilvi Pärnamägi (06/2/1939-), was only six when her parents were sent to Siberia. She became an

architect, lives in Tallinn; her husband, Helmut, died in 2015; one son.

03 Marta (1910-1931) died at age twenty-one of appendix attack.

4 Emma Rosalie "Roosi"(1874-1961), married August Kusik (1870-1953). They immigrated to New York in 1921 with their four children. Moved to The Farm in early1950s and spent their last years there.

Emma Rosalie and August Kusik's four children were:

01 John Kusik (1898-1988), executive at General Electric Co.; Vice Pres. of Chesapeake-Ohio Railroad Co., lived in Cleveland, Ohio; married *Vogue* model Gloria (where I got my middle name). They had two children.

02 Karl Kusik, also referred to as Charles (1900-1992), married Meeri Jaakson, became the Council General of Estonia in the US; returned to Estonia 1938 where became First Secretary of Foreign Affairs for the Estonian Gov.; miraculously left Estonia during first communist occupation to return to USA with family; lived in Boston area on a farm, later in California with daughter Mairi. Both Karl and wife Meeri died there. Had four children:

001 Lembit Charles Kusik "Lem" (04/24/1934-), married Wendy Palu; two adopted children; Lincoln MA

002 Mairi Janette "Sammy" (12/31/1935-), married Roger Johnson; two sons; Corte Madera, CA

003 Edgar Jan Kusik (02/21/1945-03/4/1976), not married; died at age thirty-one

004 Anne Elizabeth (06/17/1946-), married Phil Roush; two children; Oak Ridge, TN

03 Ella (1906-1965), married Max Brubaker; lived in New York City; no children

04 Erica (1909-1979), married Frank Dana, lived in New York, then near Washington, D.C., no children.

5 Martin (1876-1917), died in First World War in the Russian Czarist Army.

6 Oskar (1878-1965), worked for brother Aleksander in Tallinn; was also an evangelist. Married Anni Vilepaju; they had four children:

01 Salme (1912-2000), moved to New York in 1930s; married Valeter Rukki; they had twin sons.

02 Adele (1913-1999), married Artur Stamm; lived in Tartu; one son.

03 Viktor (04/12/1915-01/16/2001), escaped with our boat to Sweden 1944; married his university friend, Lydia Burmeister, in1946 in a double wedding ceremony with Asta Krabi (our childhood friend) and Peeter Kaups (our boat captain). Settled in Sweden where Viktor became a professor and Lydia an ear-nose-throat surgeon. Viktor and Lydia had three children.

04 Oskar "Udo" (July1922-1941-2?), had been accepted to Tartu University when in 1941 was conscripted into the Russian Army; never heard of since, died somewhere in Russia.

7 Karl Eduard "Charlie" (1883-1947), left home about age seventeen to Cardiff, Wales, worked in a boarding house for a relative; moved to Canada, later to Portland, Oregon, USA, where he owned a barber shop; married an English lady, no children.

8 Gustav Voldemar "Volli" changed name in USA to Walter (04/13/1885-12/28/1974), left home with brother Charlie for Cardiff, Wales; together to Canada; homesteaded in Alberta; worked in construction in Vancouver, BC; moved to Washington state, bought land, "The Konsa Farm" in Hockinson. Married Mary Beckman (1890-1945) who had one son, Edward, from previous marriage.

9 Maria Elisabeth "Liisbet" (1888-1974), married Gustav Luik. They owed a small grocery/variety store in Tallinn until communists confiscated it; had two daughters:

01 Astred Koidula (11/12/1923-08/1/2010), married Enno Põld, had one son from that marriage. He left her soon after the son's birth and divorced. Astred's second marriege was to Henn Ormet (05/1/1930 -); worked in a publishing firm in Tallinn where they

lived many years; died on Muhu Island where they spent several retirement years.

02 Daisy "Deps" Hellen (08/21/1928-05/10/1996), married Ermo Karjatse; schoolteacher by profession; not allowed to teach anymore when the communists arrested her husband and sent him to a slave camp in Russia; then worked in a chemical/pharmaceutical factory; lived in Tallinn; two children

10 Peter Victor "Papa Konsa" (04/29/1892-05/27/1974), minister; married Adele Marie Sünd (07/22/1901—06/29/1995); Victor and Adele Konsa had four children:

01 Hulda Marie (08/8/1929-), moved from The Farm and Portland, Oregon to Toronto; married Einar "Eino" Eistrat (02/23/1925-12/04/1999); worked in ladies' garment industry office; continues to live in Toronto, Canada; two children:

001 Allan (09/5/1953-), electronics and sound system work; not married

02 Ester Elizabeth (12/5/1930-), in Washington State became school teacher and later art teacher, married Taavi Kaups (07/22/1926-); moved to Chicago; due to husband's work they lived in Holland, England, and Sweden; traveled extensively; moved back to USA; live in Naperville, Illinois; four daughters

03 Mairy Marta Gloria (01/24/1934-), pastor's wife, administrative assistant, married Endel Meiusi

(11/07/1932-), live in Denver, Colorado; three children

04 Kaljo David "Dave" Victor (04/24/1939-), graduate of University of Washington in civil engineering, specializing in traffic and transportation; worked in that field for ten years; served in U.S. Army at Fort Ord, California; married Pamela Craise (10/18/1941-), together they moved to San Mateo, then to Los Angeles, California and back to Washington State where he became an investment advisor and where they live in Tacoma, Washington; three children

My mother's side of the family:

Hans Sünd (1840-1903), my great-grandfather, married:

Madle (Tomsen) Sünd (1839-1868), my great-grandmother. Hans had six daughters and one son. Madle, his first wife, at age twenty-eight, along with two daughters, were murdered by robbers, while the three-year-old son, Rein Sünd (my grandfather), crawled into the oven and was undetected and spared. Rein Sünd (02/23/1866-02/18/1948), my grandfather; married Maria (Sharbok) Sünd. They had one son named:

1 Leobolt, "Leo" (08/21/1887- ?), went to live in Argentina; married Beba; they had one daughter,

01 Susanna (1935-)

Leo's mother died when he was very young.

Rein Sünd (second marriage) to:

Marie (Remmelman) Sünd (02/23/1876-01/18/1948), my grandmother; Marie's father, my great-grandfather's name was:

Aadu Remmelman (05/10/1836-?), married:

Ann or Anna (Grenzmann) Remmelman (02/23/1834-?), my great-grandmother

Rein and Marie together had three children:

2 Adele Marie (07/22/1901-06/29/1995), my mother; she married Peter Victor Konsa (04/29/1892-05/27/1974), my father. They had four children (as indicated under my father's information)

3 Robert (04/23/1903-05/10/1916), died at age thirteen

4 Minda Salome (02/26/1906-12/09/1992), married Johannes "Juku" or "Juks" Rõõmus (5/15/1901-12/18/1990); owned a large farm near Ridala until the communists confiscated it; arrested both of them in 1949; Minda was sent to Tallinn to hard labor, cleaning/hauling bombed-out ruins; returned to Haapsalu and worked as a night watchman many years; four children:

01 Lehti Melinda (04/12/1927-06/21/1997), married Erich Antsve (09/1/1923-01/1/1999); educated in trade school as textile designer; worked in weaving and design and was sent all over Russia because of

her skills; also skilled in cooking; two children, lived in Haapsalu

02 Milvi Regina Rõõmus (09/05/1932-), educated in bookkeeping and worked in that field but got paid more doing piecework in a textile factory with her quick hands, which she did until retirement; not married, no children, lives in Pärnu

03 Arvi Haarald (01/12/1937-01/31/2001), twelve years old when his parents were arrested; in Russian Navy trained as a railroad technician and in electronics; worked both on the railroad and on high-powered electric lines in maintenance and repair; married Maimu Mändla - divorced, one daughter, lived near Haapsalu

04 Evi Minda (02/15/1944-), was eight when parents were arrested; married Hennu Mändla (alcoholic and abuser, divorced); electronic assembly line work and as a kindergarten food service manager; one son, lives in Haapsalu.

Contact Information

To order additional copies of this book, please visit
www.redemption-press.com.
Also available on Amazon.com and BarnesandNoble.com
Or by calling toll free 1-844-2REDEEM.

CPSIA information can be obtained
at www.ICGtesting.com
Printed in the USA
FSOW04n0550220416
19554FS